CHRISTIANITY ACCORDING TO JOHN

CHRISTIANITY ACCORDING TO JOHN

by D. George Vanderlip

 THE WESTMINSTER PRESS · PHILADELPHIA

Published by The Westminster Press ®
Philadelphia, Pennsylvania

Printed in the United States of America

Library of Congress Cataloging in Publication Data

Vanderlip, George.
   Christianity according to John.

   Bibliography: p.
   1. Bible. N.T. John—Theology. I. Title.
BS2615.2.V36   226'.5'066   74-34585
ISBN 0-664-20737-5

Contents

	PREFACE	7
1	JOHN SPEAKS TO OUR WORLD	9
2	LIFE!	31
3	JESUS AS THE WORD	46
4	OTHER TITLES FOR JESUS	58
5	THE CHILDREN OF GOD	72
6	BELIEVE	95
7	KNOW	104
8	LOVE	118
9	LIGHT AND DARKNESS	133
10	TRUTH	153
11	THE SPIRIT OF TRUTH	164
12	HISTORY AND INTERPRETATION	174
	NOTES	187
	BIBLIOGRAPHY	203
	INDEXES	217

Preface

There is a throbbing vitality to The Gospel According to John. It speaks afresh to every generation and perhaps at no time in history has there been more interest in this Gospel than now! Not only have the discoveries of the Dead Sea Scrolls and of the Gnostic documents found in Egypt contributed to this but in recent years there has emerged a new emphasis on the independent historical tradition preserved in John. There has also developed a new appreciation for the mature, in-depth understanding of the gospel and of the Christian life which The Gospel According to John presents.

This study of John has been written to provide a deeper understanding of the background and thought of the Fourth Gospel. Extensive notes and a selective bibliography have been included. At the same time, the interests of the lay reader have been kept in mind. The language and terms used are straightforward, and an effort has been made throughout not only to interpret John in the light of the time when it was written but to relate its message to the concerns of the twentieth century. All Scripture quotations, unless otherwise noted, are from the Revised Standard Version.

To the extent that these pages bring to other persons a keener insight into the content and significance of The Gospel According to John and result in a heightened awareness of the uniqueness and timeliness of its presentation of the gospel, my purpose in writing will have been achieved. To all who have been my companions in the study of the Gospel of John, I express my sincere appreciation. I am indebted to the trustees of The Eastern Baptist Theological Seminary for a recent sabbatical leave which enabled me to bring a long-cherished goal to completion. I express my thanks to the administration of Princeton Theological Seminary for granting me the status of Visiting Fellow during my sabbatical and especially for the privilege of using the magnificent resources of the Robert E. Speer Library.

To my immediate family for their constant support and encouragement I owe my heartfelt thanks and it is to them that I gratefully dedicate this book.

D. G. V.

1

~~~~~~

John Speaks
to Our World

The Gospel of John may be compared to an artesian well that never runs dry. From its depths there bubbles forth clear, refreshing water to quench the thirst of men and women who turn to it in their quest for life's true meaning. Its treasures have not yet been exhausted by the numerous books and articles that have sought to delve into and interpret its message.

The Gospel of John combines lucidity with depth. As a result, it appeals to Christians of every walk of life and of quite different backgrounds. While it speaks with force and clarity to the layman who seeks spiritual nurture and understanding, it simultaneously challenges the ingenuity and skill of professional theologians who wrestle with scores of unresolved questions about the origin, purpose, literary methodology, and history-theology blend of the Gospel of John. It is apparent that there is today a widespread interest in the Gospel of John. The continuing appearance in recent years of a flow of scholarly literature in the area of Johannine studies testifies to the heightened appreciation for the Gospel of John which now exists.

This Gospel is the product of a mature and intense

reflection upon the meaning of the coming of Jesus Christ into the world. The result is a highly developed theology with a depth interpretation of the gospel which, because of its cosmic perspective, possesses for each succeeding generation a perennial relevance to life.

A world-encompassing outlook. John's Gospel, more than any other, is the gospel with a cosmic perspective. It has a universal thrust. Jesus is "the Savior of the world" (4:42). No narrow nationalism limits the word of hope and promise. John's Gospel transcends localism and sectarianism in every form. This is a significant factor for an age that seeks ecumenicity and desperately needs international goodwill. Although the Gospel of John had its roots in the land of Israel, it is in Asia Minor that it proclaims the love of God for the world. The Gospel looks forward to the day when the separation of people will be replaced by oneness. We read, "There shall be one flock, one shepherd" (10:16).

Finding life's true meaning. We stand today in need of a reformation both like and, in many ways, unlike the one that occurred in the time of Martin Luther. We live in a time of great unrest, one that bears a number of resemblances to the restlessness of Europe in the sixteenth century. Among the problems that disturbed Luther and the people of his day was a heavy sense of guilt before God and a longing for forgiveness. In the message of the gospel as proclaimed by Paul they found the peace of soul which they sought. The apostle spoke of forgiveness "by faith alone." Luther's rediscovery of this message was the catalyst he used to reform the church of his day and to rally central Europe around him.

The problems we face are by no means identical to those of Martin Luther. Nor does it appear that the average man is greatly burdened by a sense of personal guilt. Concern about guilt has been pushed into the background by a persistent questioning about the meaning and purpose of life in general. There is a struggle with the apparent meaninglessness of life and along with this a rebellion, on the part of youth especially, against the established order. They ask such questions as: Why are things the way they are? Why do poverty, injustice, and inequity mar so much of modern society?

Youth are concerned with questions like these: Where can we discover firm values by which to live, and meaningful ideals for which to strive? How can we find justice in a world of widespread prejudice, and equity in a society in which privilege exists for only the very few? Youth seek a path in a jungle of unrest, a light in the gloomy upheaval of uncertainty and hate. Reality, genuineness, and truth—these are the concerns that grip the hearts of young men and women who are struggling for identity.

Can the message of the Gospel of John speak convincingly to these burning questions? The present study will seek to respond creatively to these crucial issues.

The Relevance of the Gospel of John Today

In our day when there is this sense of hopelessness and despair which envelops so many serious-minded persons, John's quotation in the words of Jesus, "I have come that men may have life, and may have it in all its fullness" (John 10:10b, NEB), seems particularly relevant. People are finding that life's true significance is not contained in the latest product rolling off the assembly line or in some highly advertised discovery. Life's meaning is tied to God and to our relationship to him, not to things. Such relationship may or may not include hardship and suffering. In the case of Jesus, his obedience to the will of God led to the cross. This seeming tragedy did not make his style of life any less the "abundant life" or "life in all its fullness." In fact, his death for others was the clearest demonstration of the reality of his message. He said,

Truly, truly, I say to you, unless a grain of wheat falls into the earth and dies, it remains alone; but if it dies, it bears much fruit. (12:24)

The cross, in other words, did not negate Jesus' message but dramatically and forever confirmed it. The cross *is* the message. He came not to be served but to serve. In the act of foot washing, two lessons are contained.[1] (1) It is presented as a prophetic action symbolizing Jesus' death in humiliation for the salvation of others (13:2-11). (2) It is an example of the humility which followers of Jesus are to imitate (13:12-20).

Freedom, truth, and love. There are many aspects to the abundant life that Jesus proclaimed. Included in the central qualities of this new life are freedom, truth, and love.

Jesus said, "So if the Son makes you free, you will be free indeed" (8:36). In our day there is a call for freedom around the world. This call is not religious in the restricted meaning of the word, and yet when men are in bondage it is impossible to ignore the spiritual dimensions of this injustice. If religion has to do with man's deepest and innermost concerns, then the problems of bondage and oppression are inevitably religious as well as social and political issues. Not only do nations strive for independence but the oppressed and disenfranchised peoples of the world, in whatever country or community they live, raise their hands in yearning and in struggle for liberation.

Traditionally, we have interpreted the freedom that Jesus speaks about as the deliverance from sin, and this is both valid and normative. Does it exhaust the message of Jesus, however, to understand the significance of his coming among men in this way? Is there not in his message a broader freedom that sometimes escapes us? Do we not see in his willingness, for example, to talk at length with the socially ostracized Samaritan woman an inescapable proclamation of social concern and outreach? The woman was rejected by the Jews because of her ethnic ancestry and religion, and by her own people because of her libertinism. By his association with her, Jesus broke with tradition. He displayed an acceptance of her as a person which should carry for us far-reaching implications. Nationality, race, religion, morals, poverty, ignorance, sex, age, social customs—*none* of these can properly remain barriers between peoples of the earth. The love and concern of God reaches to the farthest, the neediest, and the humblest persons. That love reaches them through disciples who have heeded and responded to the message of Jesus. If God accepts such men and women, then we, who claim to be children of God, can do no less. The social implications of the message and life-style of our Lord, proclaimed both by word and by deed, remain as a persistent challenge to the recalcitrant prejudices and callous bigotry of modern man. The gospel liberates! If truly heeded, it can be the catalyst to bring fulfillment to the dreams of liberty which pulsate within the hearts of people everywhere.

Along with the contemporary cry for freedom is the demand for genuineness and truth. The facade and cant of much of modern life have led to a widespread desire for something real, genuine, and honest. This quest for reality versus sham, for that which is reliable and valid versus so much that is empty and meaningless, is fruitful soil for the proclamation of the good news concerning Jesus Christ, who is "the truth" (14:6) and whose "life was the light of men" (1:4). He is "the true light" (1:9) and "the true vine" (15:1). When so many in our day share the despairing mood of atheistic existentialism and some turn to drugs or the occult in search of meaning, we will do well to continue to proclaim the message of the gospel of Jesus Christ as heralded in the Gospel of John. There Jesus is unequivocally presented as the one who has brought light and life to men.

Included in John's message is the new commandment that

Jesus' followers love one another. While a dearth of feeling for other people has characterized human civilization since its beginning, there is today a persistent cry for genuine concern for others. The consciences of Christians are being stirred as never before by this imperative. Sometimes the cry for love emerges in distorted forms, as in the current plea for free love and communal family living. These expressions usually collapse under the weight of their own excesses and unnaturalness. Sometimes the desire for love is expressed in the more sophisticated philosophy of situational ethics. In whatever form this need for love emerges, it testifies to a deep-felt human longing and necessity. John makes love normative and foundational for all Christian ethics. For John, love does not remain an abstract human emotion. His understanding of love involves *creative human response to need.* This meaning is derived more from a study of what is said in I John than from the Gospel of John. In I John 3:18 we find the words, "Little children, let us not love in word or speech but in deed and in truth." The word "pragmatic" might be used to describe John's emphasis on love. This word is derived from the Greek word *prassein,* meaning "to do." John states that love will issue in *actions* of goodwill and service. Love, for John, is not restricted to some amorphous and volatile emotion. It is a quality of interpersonal relationships and is demonstrated by deeds of kindness and by acts of concern.

If there is one criticism that could be leveled at this point against the Gospel of John, it is that the author did not express more clearly and forcefully the fact that Christian *agapē* (i.e., love) reaches beyond the Christian fellowship to those as yet outside the church. God's love for the world is clearly stated in the book (3:16), but in the instruction to the disciples, perhaps because of the stress and struggle for survival of the church at that time, it appears that in the author's mind love within the fellowship dominated his thinking. Of course, Christian love could well be said to begin there, but if Christ gave his life for the world, then Christian love as seen in the lives of the disciples can be no less universal in its outreach than the love of God himself. Here other parts of the New Testament canon can help to supplement the treatment of this theme as found in the Fourth Gospel.

God's continuing revelation of his will. We have noted, up to this point, that John's emphases consistently transcend geographic and ethnic barriers. It may be emphasized further that the author frees the gospel from any view which would anchor God's activity exclusively in the past. It is true that God spoke in history in Jesus Christ, but it is of fully equal importance that through the Holy Spirit, God *continues* to speak to his church. The Holy Spirit is the Paraclete and the Spirit of Truth. As such he is sent by Jesus Christ and comes as the Spirit of Christ. It is the function of the Spirit to continue the work of Jesus and to guide the disciples into the fuller truth which they were not prepared to receive when Jesus was with them (14:26; 16:13). The Spirit is God's means of leading men and women into ever new and fresh insights into the meanings, implications, and imperatives of the gospel. In this we see the present, dynamic activity of God. How effectively this proclamation counters the pessimistic perspective of a philosophy that posits a dead or absent God! Here is an invitation to faith over against unfaith. Here is a message of courage as opposed to one of fear.

The Gospel of John can itself be viewed as the prime example of the work of the Spirit as he continues to lead the Christian community after the resurrection and the ascension of Jesus Christ our Lord. The grasp of the meaning of Jesus in history as presented by the author of the Fourth Gospel transcends the understanding that the disciples had during Jesus' earthly ministry. He has pondered the events that have transpired and he has both discussed them within the community of believers and proclaimed them to the world. In interpreting the awesome advent of the Son of God among the sons of men, he has had the inner guidance of the Spirit of God. The result has been the proclamation of a message that, despite its emergence in a Jewish-Palestinian milieu, has been molded into new cosmic and cosmopolitan dimensions. John's forceful proclamation of the presence and activity of God in the world encourages us to pursue with confidence God's solution to the quandaries that trouble man and society in the challenging years of the twentieth century. To us too, as to Christians of the first century, there comes the assurance of the instruction and guidance of the Spirit of Truth.

This book focuses on the theology of John and approaches it through the study of individual themes. Because of the interrelated nature of many of the Johannine topics there will inevitably be a close relationship between the separate chapters. It is hoped that each will shed light on the others.

The Writer's Purpose

In studying the Gospel of John, we need to consider at the outset what the author's purpose was when he wrote. This can be discovered in two ways. The first approach is to examine what he himself specifically states regarding his purpose. The second method is to analyze the contents of the book itself.

Let us begin by considering John's own declaration of purpose as given in John 20:30–31, which reads,

Now Jesus did many other signs in the presence of the disciples, which are not written in this book; but these are written that you may believe that Jesus is the Christ, the Son of God, and that believing you may have life in his name.

This statement contains three basic affirmations:

1. The author's central message is related to Jesus, whom he presents to his readers as "the Christ, the Son of God."

2. There is an appeal for "believing" in Jesus. This concept carries for John the connotation of trust and commitment as well as of intellectual assent to a statement of fact.

3. The result of such a personal and positive response will be "life" in his name.

Upon our examination of the affirmation of purpose that the author himself has given, what should we say is his central theme? Some have suggested *Christology* (i.e., the nature and person of Christ), others *faith*, and still others *life*. To stress faith as the key to the Gospel of John has certain weaknesses. First of all, the noun "faith" never appears in the Gospel. Only the verb "to believe" is used. Secondly, John never emphasizes the concept of believing per se. For him, believing always has an object, namely, Jesus Christ. Thirdly, and crucially, believing for John is only the means and not the end that the writer has in view. The goal he has in mind is "life." Therefore, to call the Gospel of John "The Gospel of Belief," or even "The Gospel of Believing," is inadequate. Although it has the merits of focusing on an important aspect of John's message, it fails to highlight what is most essential in his presentation.

A strong case can be made for calling John "The Gospel of Life." Life is clearly a prominent and consistent emphasis throughout the Gospel. A key verse in this regard would be John 10:10, "I came that they may have life, and have it abundantly." "Life," for John, is not, however, an independent possession or quality, unrelated to God or to Jesus Christ. The author writes, "And this is eternal life, that they know thee the only true God, and Jesus Christ whom thou hast sent" (17:3). "Life," as John uses the word, involves a God-man relationship of fellowship and communion. When this is present, then personal well-being and spiritual whole-ness become possible. The knowledge of God, in other words, is the key to the meaning of eternal life. Knowledge, as it is referred to here, implies fellowship as well as intellectual understanding. The suggested title, "The Gospel of Life," then, when understood with John's meaning of "life," has much to commend it.

This leads us to consider the third element found in the declaration of purpose, namely, Christology. The author writes, "These are written that you may believe that Jesus is the Christ, the Son of God." The addition of the words "the Son of God" is not to be viewed as of secondary importance. While Jesus is presented as the Christ (a Greek translation of the Hebrew term, Messiah), it is clear that John's message reaches beyond Jewish hopes and is one that is for all. The fulfillment of the hope of Israel in the coming of the Messiah is presented by John in such a way as to make it clear that the good news he proclaims is for all people everywhere. The expression "the Son of God" does not focus primarily on Jewish expectations of a national deliverer, but rather on the fact that Jesus has come from the Father and that in him God has manifested himself in the world.

It should be noted that Jesus always points beyond himself to the Father (14:9–11). Consequently it would be proper to say that at the heart of John's Christology is *theology*. (In Greek, *theos* means "God.") God is central to John's whole message.

God has manifested himself in the world through the Son.

> And the Word became flesh and dwelt among us, full of grace and truth; we have beheld his glory, glory as of the only Son from the Father. (1:14)

It is for the purpose of *revelation* that the Son has come. He came to reveal the Father. In and through the coming of the Christ the divine presence has entered the world and has made spiritual life a possibility for all persons. Perhaps the Johannine perspective on divine presence accounts for the shift of emphasis in John from a future hope to the present realization of the Spirit. The miracle to be shared is the reality of God's presence with men—first in Jesus Christ and then in the Paraclete, who, as the Spirit of Truth, continues the ministry of Jesus. In Christ and in the Spirit, God has manifested himself to men and continues to do so. This is the message of John.

An examination of the contents of the Gospel of John shows that, apart from the passion narrative, most of it consists of two main elements, namely, miracles (usually referred to as "signs") and discourses. These two diverse components share a common purpose, however; that is, to instruct the readers concerning the person of Jesus Christ and to lead to a positive response of faith in him. It would be valid to call both of these major segments of John's Gospel Christocentric. Both focus primarily on Jesus as the Christ, the Son of God. The readers are prepared for this emphasis by the Prologue which first introduced this theme.

In the light of our study of the author's statement of purpose and of the contents of the Gospel, perhaps the best subtitle we could give to the Gospel of John would be "The Gospel of the Son of God." This designation puts the emphasis on the Son as the revealer of God, which is fitting, since, as we have seen, this is really the heart of John's message.

The expression "the Son of God" is often replaced in the body of the Gospel by a wide variety of terms, such as "the Logos," "the Christ," "the Son," "the one whom God has sent," "the bread which came down from heaven." These are but different ways of presenting John's message. This is the good news of the Gospel. Jesus is the Son of God. He has made God known, and through him eternal life can be ours.

INTENDED READERS

We might expect general agreement about the destination and intended readers of the Gospel of John, but this is not the case. The wide range of opinions on the matter is illustrated by the fact that some men, such as C. H. Dodd,[2] have argued that the book was written primarily to convince educated Greeks in cosmopolitan centers that Jesus is the Son of God. Prof. W. C. van Unnik,[3] on the other hand, has maintained that the intended readers were Jews of the Diaspora and Gentiles attending the synagogues whom the author is seeking to win to the Christian church. Both of these interpreters of the Fourth Gospel would agree that the primary purpose in the mind of the author was evangelism, that is to say, to win converts; in the one case they would be educated Greeks, in the other, Diaspora Jews primarily. According to both authors, the readers reside outside of Palestine.

Other interpreters, such as C. K. Barrett, E. Hoskyns and F. N. Davey, and Raymond E. Brown, maintain that evangelism was not the primary concern of the author and that the instruction of the church was central in his mind. The intended readers were Christians of the churches of Asia Minor who needed to have their faith strengthened. C. K. Barrett has written:

> The profundity of the gospel is such that it seems very doubtful whether anyone, however intelligent, who had not a good grounding in the gospel tradition and elementary Christian theology would appreciate it.[4]

The conclusion of E. Hoskyns and F. N. Davey was that "the Gospel was written pastorally for Christians and polemically against Jews." [5] This view is shared by Raymond E. Brown, who writes:

> John's attitude toward "the Jews" is not missionary but apologetic and polemic. . . . The decisive theological em-

phases in the Gospel . . . are directed to crises within the believing Church rather than to the conversion of non-believers.[6]

As to whether the original readers of the Fourth Gospel were Jews or Greeks, it seems best to conclude that Christians of both backgrounds were included. It can be shown that there are aspects of John's Gospel which indicate that the readers were not unfamiliar with the Old Testament. At the same time, the explanation of such commonplace terms as "Rabbi," "Messiah," and "Passover" suggests that among the readers are some for whom these terms are strange and unfamiliar.[7] People of Gentile background would appear to be in the author's mind at this point. The fact that the Gospel speaks both to persons who have considerable knowledge of the Old Testament and to persons who are ignorant of elementary Jewish terminology suggests that the book is addressed to both Jewish and Gentile readers. The church by this time in the first century had a mixed membership. Gentiles had been welcomed into a fellowship that began with a Jewish nucleus. It is not at all surprising, therefore, that the author of the Fourth Gospel addresses Christian readers of both backgrounds as he writes.

THE ARGUMENTS FOR A PRIMARILY CHRISTIAN READERSHIP

Several arguments can be advanced to support the view that the Gospel of John was written primarily for Christian believers. We shall list some of the more cogent of these.

1. *The Synoptics.* The Gospel of John assumes much that is contained in the Synoptic Gospels. The most convincing explanation for this is that the writer is aware that the readers already know the basic story of the life and ministry of Jesus. Only about 8 percent of the Gospel of John repeats what is found in the accounts of Matthew, Mark, and Luke. John's

readers may or may not have read the Synoptics. They could have gained their knowledge from Christian preaching. The significant factor is, however, that John felt no need to repeat much that was of basic interest in the life of Jesus. Clearly, his readers already know the essential facts. Their source of knowledge could have been written, or oral, or a combination of both. In any case, they were not hearing the Christian message for the first time.

2. *Church concerns.* A large portion of the Gospel is directed specifically to concerns that relate to the church. Much of it consists of material in which non-Christian Jews or Greeks would have little interest. This is singularly true in the case of the farewell discourses found in chs. 13 to 17. Here the instruction concerns the need for unity in the church, the command to love the brethren, the promise of the gift of the Holy Spirit, and other diverse exhortations for believers. All these elements are appropriate in a document intended to instruct Christians but would be rather incongruous in a book prepared primarily for evangelistic outreach.

3. *"The Jews."* The attitude toward the Jews found in the Gospel of John can hardly be described as either winsome or conciliatory. The suggestion of W. C. van Unnik that this is an evangelistic document aimed at Diaspora Jews fails to account adequately for this fact. The Gospel of John is more of an apologetic *against* Judaism than a persuasive narrative likely to win converts from among the representatives of this faith. "The Jews," as a corporate entity, are consistently cast in an unfavorable light. The various objections of official Judaism to Christian claims appear to have been gathered by the author and he has attempted to answer them systematically in chs. 7 and 8. In his doing so, it would seem that his interest goes beyond that which is purely historical. The arguments against Christ to which he addresses himself should, in all probability, be viewed as incorporating not only

those which the Jews of Jesus' day advanced against him but also some of the objections which the Jews of Asia Minor were currently raising against Christian beliefs as well. In other words, the author has taken this opportunity to give counsel to his fellow Christians who, with him, face the responsibility of replying to the objections of contemporary Jews to the church's affirmations concerning Jesus of Nazareth. It could be argued that an apology of this nature could well, in its own way, serve evangelistic purposes. The answers to the Jewish objections to Jesus, as given in this Gospel, would be useful to the Christian community in its efforts to enter into dialogue with the Jews of their time. It could, indeed, serve as a kind of *apologia* and perhaps prove itself to be an effective evangelistic instrument. This indirect use of the Gospel for evangelism, however, is something quite distinct from the suggestion that this Gospel was written primarily as a document to be put into the hands of Jews in order to bring them to a Christian confession. Such a direct use in Jewish evangelism has not to date been satisfactorily demonstrated.

4. *John the Baptist.* In John there exists what appears to be a corrective to a current view regarding the role of John the Baptist. The Gospel consistently depicts John as subordinate to Jesus: "He was not the light, but came to bear witness to the light" (1:8). Were there some who at that time argued that it was John the Baptist who was the light of men? We know that John the Baptist also had disciples (3:25). In Acts 19:1–7 a group is described which appears to have retained a peculiar loyalty to him. Was the author of the Gospel of John seeking to emphasize that John the Baptist's role must be viewed as preparatory and therefore secondary to the position of Jesus? There seems to be some justification for entertaining this conclusion.

5. *Gnosticism.* The vocabulary of John bears a resemblance to the vocabulary found in Gnostic documents.

Gnosticism was a religious movement that was strongly dualistic and held as one of its views that Jesus only appeared to have a human body. Some see in ch. 1:14 an argument against the Gnostic view, but this verse has been variously interpreted.

> And the Word became flesh and dwelt among us, full of grace and truth; we have beheld his glory, glory as of the only Son from the Father.

Clearly anti-Gnostic statements are found in I John 4:2–3 and II John 7.

Although Gnosticism did not become a developed and recognizable system of thought until the second century, some of the doctrines that would later characterize Gnosticism were already present at the time John wrote. John strove to correct what, in his judgment, was a grievous error, for it denied the true humanity of Jesus. When we think of this corrective emphasis, and of the one we noted with regard to John the Baptist, it is evident that in both cases we are dealing with problems that would concern, primarily, Christians rather than non-Christians. The views he opposed were regarded as heresies which seriously misrepresented the person and significance of Jesus. It is in answer to these threats that the author took the time to deliver his words of warning and of instruction. The relationship of John to Gnosticism will receive fuller discussion in a separate chapter.

6. *The Epilogue.* In the Epilogue (ch. 21) reference is made to the martyrdom of Peter and seemingly to the death of the beloved disciple. While this chapter may well have been written some time after the rest of the book had been completed, there is no evidence that the Gospel as a whole was ever published without the Epilogue. It would have been *within* the Christian fellowship that both the martyrdom of Peter and the death of the beloved disciple would have been of serious concern. In the case of the latter, the author's

statement regarding his death and what Jesus had had to say about it may well have been prompted by a popular current opinion that this disciple would not die before the second coming of Christ. The reference to the martyrdom of these disciples would be of interest to Christian readers only. 7. *I John*. When John and I John are compared carefully, it becomes evident that there is not only a remarkable similarity of vocabulary between them, but that there is also a strong resemblance between their subject matters. The same themes dominate in each. The similarity of the two writings is of such a nature as to suggest that the situations in which and for which they both were written were more or less identical. The intended readers of both could very well have been the same. It is clear that I John was written to Christians and not to non-Christians. The Gospel of John is sufficiently similar to the First Letter of John to make it plausible that we have to do with either an identical readership or at least with readers who are very similar in their ideas and needs. If it is true that each of these works emerges from the same milieu, then it should be recognized, more widely than it actually is, that the best commentary we can have on the Gospel of John is the First Letter of John. Much that is obscure in the Gospel can have light shed on it from the Letter, for the life setting of the latter is more readily discernible than is that of the Gospel.

While in the Gospel of John we can catch only a glimpse of the writer's immediate environment, in I John we can discern a community of Christians, contemporary with the author, to whom the exhortation is directly addressed. It would seem to be defensible to say that the Gospel of John gives to I John a theology and that I John gives to the Gospel of John a "home." They complement each other. To those who did not separate themselves from the group but remained faithful the author speaks words of consolation and he says regarding those who have chosen to withdraw that they actually never really belonged to the redemptive circle in the first place. Their subsequent departure is patent proof of their lack of commitment and sincerity (I John 2:19). They had not attained to the unity of the fellowship through the Spirit, for they never really had shared in the birth through the Spirit. Hence their withdrawal. This experience of schism helps to explain why it is that there is such a stress on the unity of the church in the Gospel of John (17:20–23). The departure of some professed believers from the group has apparently caused a certain anxiety within the Christian community. Consequently, the author feels compelled to emphasize the importance of Christian unity. Perhaps the need for unity and for steadfastness motivated the author's inclusion of Peter's answer to the question of Jesus, "Will you also go away?" (6:67) Peter replies:

> Lord, to whom shall we go? You have the words of eternal life; and we have believed, and have come to know, that you are the Holy One of God. (6:68–69)

The recording of Peter's profession of faith and of his fidelity may well have been intended as an example for all believers.

In summary, it may be said that the Gospel of John was written for Christians, both Jews and Gentiles, who needed to be encouraged in their faith in the face of opposition and of various errors.

ORIGIN, DATE, AND AUTHORSHIP

As to the place of origin of this Gospel, the traditional suggestion of Ephesus has as much to commend it as any alternative that has been advanced. It appears that we have in this Gospel a message which originated in Palestine and which is now being reexpressed in a Hellenistic, cosmopolitan center in Asia Minor.

No specific date for the appearance of John can be

affirmed without question. A date late in the first century is most commonly suggested. We possess a fragment of an early copy of the Gospel of John which has been dated at approximately A.D. 125. The Gospel was presumedly written some decades earlier. I would incline toward a date about A.D. 85–90 in view of the references to excommunication from the synagogue (9:22; 12:42; 16:2). Such an official decree against Jewish Christians appears to be the product of the Jamnia academy about A.D. 85.[8]

The Gospel of John preserves an independent tradition of the ministry of Christ. As a result the historical value of the Gospel has received new attention in recent years. It continues to be viewed primarily as a theological interpretation of the life and ministry of Christ, but it is not without several significant reminiscences which give evidence of being rooted in a valid historical tradition. This matter of history and interpretation will receive further discussion in a subsequent chapter.

The book is anonymous and the matter of authorship remains unsettled. The Johannine literature of the New Testament seems to be the product of a group, a "school" of theological thought, which has certain distinctive emphases. Perhaps this school has its origin through the dynamic preaching and personality of John, the Son of Zebedee, as tradition suggests. Friends and disciples helped to shape a nucleus of material that came to them in the form of preaching and teaching presented, molded, and handed down over a period of many years. That a group is involved in this literature is suggested by both internal and external evidence. In the Gospel we have a group endorsement of the contents of the book in the statement,

This is the disciple who is bearing witness to these things, and who has written these things; and we know that his testimony is true. (21:24)

Also there has been preserved in Eusebius a tradition based on a statement by Clement of Alexandria (fl. A.D. 190–200):

> John, last of all, conscious that the outward facts had been set forth in the Gospels, was urged on by his disciples, and, divinely moved by the Spirit, composed a spiritual Gospel.[9]

The inclusion of the phrase "urged on by his disciples" supports the suggestion of a group clustered around the author. The beloved disciple, to whom the book is attributed (21:20–24), appears, however, not to have been living when the Gospel of John was finally published. Chapter 21 at least reflects a knowledge of his death. The inclusion of the discussion between Jesus and the beloved disciple and the explanation of the meaning of that discussion as given in the Epilogue (ch. 21) indicates the church's need to be reassured that Jesus had not promised that this disciple would live until the time of Christ's return to earth. Such a rumor had apparently gained some credence. Therefore the statement is made:

> Yet Jesus did not say to him that he was not to die, but, "If it is my will that he remain until I come, what is that to you?" (21:23)

Could it be that the Gospel had its origin in the oral preaching and teaching of the beloved disciple, and that various friends and disciples of his helped to put it into its present form?

The original draft of the Gospel must have ended with ch. 20, for the statement of purpose in 20:30–31 brought the book to a proper close. When ch. 21 was added, the earlier chapters apparently went through editorial modification. The same kind of group endorsement found in 21:24 occurs in 19:34 following the reference to the fact that when Jesus' side was pierced there came out "blood and water." The comment reads:

He who saw it has borne witness—his testimony is true, and
he knows that he tells the truth—that you also may believe.
(19:35)

Furthermore, the original draft of the farewell discourses may
have included only chs. 13 and 14.[10] The sequence between
chs. 14 and 15 is unnatural. Jesus says, "I will no longer talk
much with you" (14:30) and yet three long chapters of
discourse follow. Also, the chapter ends with the words,
"Rise, let us go hence" (14:31) and there is no indication that
they move from the room.

When chs. 14 and 18 are placed in sequence there appears
to be a smooth and natural transition. The awkwardness of
14:31 suggests that the person who added chs. 15 through 17
felt that the material already written down should not be
modified. It was already held in such high regard that there
was no inclination to alter it in any way.

One possible summary of the history of the development of
the Fourth Gospel might well be the following:

1. It finds its origin and inspiration in the oral preaching
and teaching of the beloved disciple.

2. A disciple and friend prepares a first draft of the Gospel
based on the beloved disciple's proclamations.

3. A subsequent editor (or editors) prepares an enlarged
draft by incorporating such supplementary materials as chs.
15 to 17 and 21. Probably certain other modifications may
have been made to the original work before the Gospel was
finally published for public reading in the churches. Since all
manuscripts that have survived reflect only the full Gospel as
we now have it, it seems safe to suggest that any expansion of
an earlier draft that may have taken place must have
occurred prior to the public release of the Gospel. There
seems never to have been circulated a shorter form of this
Gospel. By the time it was issued it existed essentially as we
have it now. There were, of course, some subsequent scribal

additions, such as the reference to the angel stirring the water annually at the pool of Bethesda (5:4) and the account of the woman detected in adultery (7:53 to 8:11). The origin of these additions, however, can be explained as late scribal glosses and are not of the same character as the creative editorial formulation that we have posited for the Gospel as a whole.

2

~~~~~~~~~~~~~~~~~~~~~~~~~~~~

Life!

The most encompassing and significant word in the Gospel of John is *life*. The author says that the purpose of writing the book was so that persons might find life through Jesus Christ (20:30,31). Jesus, in this Gospel, defines his ministry in terms of bringing persons "abundant life" or "life in fullness" (10:10). Jesus is the source of "living water" (4:10).

The importance and meaning of life in John. The term "life" occurs thirty-two times in the Prologue and the Book of Signs (chs. 2 to 12), where Jesus manifests himself to the world. It is found only three times in the Book of the Passion (chs. 13 to 20) and the Epilogue. "Life" is the message of hope offered to those who believe. When the book comes to ch. 13, Jesus is with "his own" and it is assumed that those to whom Jesus speaks in the farewell discourses (chs. 13 to 17) have already exercised such faith. Consequently they have come to possess life and therefore the subject matter of the book advances to other themes. In the farewell discourses Jesus gives final instructions to his disciples, speaks about the meaning of his

31

death, gives exhortations regarding humility, love, being witnesses, abiding in Christ, the need for unity, the gift of the Spirit, and he promises that the disciples will someday be with Christ to behold his glory in the presence of the Father.

One of the most comprehensive and thorough studies on the theme of "life" is that by Franz Mussner.[1] He argues quite convincingly that in Johannine theology life is the totality of salvation which God imparts through Jesus Christ to those who believe. Life for John means to become a child of God through a birth of the Spirit, to pass from death to life, from darkness to light, and from bondage to freedom. With the reception of life comes the experience of the love of God, and the gifts of joy and peace. To the believer is given the Holy Spirit to strengthen, teach, and guide him and to assure him victory over the persecutions of the world and the power of the devil. Involved is the forgiveness of sins and fellowship with Christ and with the Father. This life is a present reality and it will reach its consummation in a fuller dimension in the Father's house when all believers will be with Christ and see his glory.

The word "life" is much more prominent in John than it is in the Synoptic Gospels, as the following frequency list indicates:

	Matt.	Mark	Luke	John	I John
$z\bar{o}\bar{e}$ ("life")	7	4	5	35	13

John uses $z\bar{o}\bar{e}$ ("life") and $z\bar{o}\bar{e}$ $ai\bar{o}nios$ ("eternal life") interchangeably. They are for him equivalents. He shows no real preference for either expression, for he uses "life" eighteen times and "eternal life" seventeen times in his Gospel. John places the two expressions in parallel constructions. The addition of the adjective "eternal" adds no distinguishable difference in meaning. Examples of parallel constructions are the following:

He who believes in the Son has *eternal life;* he who does not obey the Son shall not see *life,* but the wrath of God rests upon him. (3:36)

You search the scriptures, because you think that in them you have *eternal life;* and it is they that bear witness to me; yet you refuse to come to me that you may have *life.* (5:39–40)

The same equivalency is apparent in I John, where "life" is used seven times and "eternal life" is found in six places. They are placed parallel to each other in these passages:

The *life* was made manifest, and we saw it, and testify to it, and proclaim to you the *eternal life* which was with the Father and was made manifest to us. (I John 1:2)

And this is the testimony, that God gave us *eternal life,* and this *life* is in his Son. (I John 5:11)

"Life" is primarily a qualitative term in John. It speaks of a new quality of existence so radically different from what a man experiences without it that its opposite can be called "death" (5:24). The addition of the adjective "eternal" does not change the meaning of "life" from a qualitative to a quantitative one. By its very nature it cannot cease to exist. It cannot come to an end. But that is not the primary meaning of the adjective *aiōnios* as John uses it. It refers to the "life of the age to come," which has already now entered time and become a part of the spiritual experience of the believer. Since the adjective bears this richer and more comprehensive connotation, it is certainly better to translate it as "eternal" than as "everlasting." "Everlasting" is a quantitative term. It simply states that something will endure forever. It fails to express the richer overtones of the blessings of the promised messianic age that are implied by the word. The adjective "eternal," on the other hand, is broad enough in its meaning to include both the qualitative and the quantitative connotations of life. It is interesting to note that the translators of the King James Version rendered the adjective as "everlasting" on eight occasions and as "eternal" the other nine times that it occurs in John. A uniform translation is to be preferred.

The prominence given "life" in John. As noted earlier, Christ's mission is epitomized by the words:

> I came that they may have life, and have it abundantly. (10:10)

The word here rendered "abundantly" *(perissos)* carries such meanings as "extraordinary," "remarkable," "profuse," "in abundance," "more than sufficient." The New English Bible expresses the thought well with the translation:

> I have come that men may have life, and may have it *in all its fullness.* (10:10, NEB)

This is life as God intended it to be. It is complete and perfect, overflowing and lacking in nothing. It is life in fellowship with God. In fact, it is this vital relationship to God through Jesus Christ that is the very essence of the life which John describes (17:3; cf. I John 1:2–3).

For John, life is inseparable from God and from Jesus Christ, whom he sent into the world. In the Logos was life and this life was the light of men (1:4). To the Son it was granted that he have life in himself (5:26). Christ gives "the living water" (4:10), he is "the bread of life" (6:35), he has the words of eternal life (6:68), and he is himself the resurrection and the life (11:25). He is the way, the truth, and the life (14:6) and gives life to whom he will (5:21).

The signs and discourses of the first twelve chapters all serve to focus on the theme of life. The Book of Signs presents as its final and climactic sign the raising of Lazarus from the dead (ch. 11). Here is the supreme demonstration that Jesus is "the life-giver." The resuscitation of Lazarus is not in itself the gift of eternal life. Lazarus' resurrection simply reveals the power of God and illustrates the eternal life which Jesus gives. Similarly "the bread from heaven" which is Jesus is illustrated by the multiplying of the loaves and the fish (ch. 6). Lazarus would die physically again. The eternal life which Christ gives is imperishable (11:25–26). Life is a unifying theme which ties the entire Gospel together. It was in order that men might find life that the book was written (20:30–31). Because of the prominence and pervasiveness of the theme of life in The Gospel According to John it has appropriately been given the name "The Gospel of life." [2]

Zōē ("life") versus psychē ("soul") in John. In English translations another Greek word in addition to zōē is rendered "life," namely, psychē. This word is found ten times in The Gospel According to John and twice in I John. Psychē refers to the soul or self as the seat and center of the inner life of man (12:25,27) or it can describe one's physical life on earth (10:11,15,17; 13:37–38; 15:13; I John 3:16). These uses do not refer to the "life" which Christ brings. To express this idea John uses only the word zōē. When Jesus gives up his "life" (10:11,15,17) the Greek word used is appropriately psychē, for the meaning is Jesus' earthly life. Jesus does not give up his zōē, for it is imperishable.

"Life" and salvation. In John's Gospel "eternal life" and salvation are placed parallel to each other, thereby implying that for the writer they are regarded as equivalents. Note the following examples:

For God so loved the world that he gave his only Son, that whoever believes in him should not perish but have *eternal life.* For God sent the Son into the world, not to condemn the world, but that the world might be *saved* through him. (3:16–17)

I am the door; if any one enters by me, he will be *saved,* and will go in and out and find pasture. The thief comes only to steal and kill and destroy; I came that they may have *life,* and have it abundantly. (10:9–10)

For John, "life" is the term he uses to describe the salvation which Jesus brings to humanity. The statement by E. Smilde seems, therefore, to be accurate:

> We can . . . define life, according to John's conception, as the totality of salvation which God in Christ imparts to the sinner through faith.
>
> With respect to its contents, life means deliverance from perdition, from the wrath and judgment of God and from death. It fulfills the deepest needs of men.[3]

Life for John as a present possession. John does not think of life as something that is promised to believers and that they will inherit someday. It is for them an experience and a reality from the moment they believe.

He who believes in the Son has eternal life (3:36). He has it not as a promise but as a present possession. He has passed from death to life (5:24). In place of estrangement and disobedience, there has come openness and spiritual communion between the creature and the Creator. This has been made possible through Jesus, who reveals the Father and who is "the way, and the truth, and the life" (14:6). This new quality of life begins when a person responds to the message of the good news through believing. John challenges his readers not to place all their hopes and expectations on the distant future when Jesus will come again, for thereby they will fail to appreciate and appropriate what is already theirs in the gift of life from the Son of God. Perhaps the delay in the expected second coming made this emphasis in John necessary and especially relevant. Disappointment and disillusionment were attitudes that had to be faced and countered. John's approach is positive and affirming. Christ has given us life and by the gift of his Spirit he is already with us. Therefore joy and peace and victory rightfully belong to us. For John, believers already possess in the present time the salvation of the age to come. The life of the age to come has moved out of the future into the present. The future will simply bring to consummation and completion the eternal life which is already a present possession. The crisis of existence comes with the decision a person makes regarding Jesus. To believe in him results in the gift of life. Not to believe brings about the consequence of remaining in darkness, death, and judgment (3:18-19; 5:24). As a result physical death is of fading significance for the believer. It is simply the moving from one degree of fellowship with God to a fuller realization and enjoyment of it in the age to come. Therefore it is stated:

> Father, I desire that they also, whom thou hast given me, may be with me where I am, to behold my glory which thou hast given me in thy love for me before the foundation of the world. (17:24)

> Beloved, we are God's children now; it does not yet appear what we shall be, but we know that when he appears we shall be like him, for we shall see him as he is. (I John 3:2)

Other passages in John that stress the present aspect of eternal life are the following: 3:15-16; 6:40,47,53,54,68; 10:28; and 17:2-3.

Salvation, for John, is not only a deliverance from sin and judgment but a radical transformation and enrichment of existence. It implies fellowship with God. It involves the experience of the unification of one's life. The believer becomes united with Christ, with the Father, and with fellow believers. All of this is integrally related to his acknowledgment of the Lordship of Jesus. The gift of life implies growth and fruitfulness. The branches of the vine will be fruitful if they remain connected with the vine. Discipleship is not complete with a crisis experience of commitment. Initial affirmation of the Lordship of Jesus is but the beginning of a life with God. John writes in order to lead his readers into a new appropriation of the Spirit and to encourage them to rise to higher plateaus of Christian experience in such crucial areas as love, unity, witness, faithfulness in persecution, humble service to one another, the ministry of teaching, and the experience of Jesus' gifts of peace and joy.

Life for John as also a future inheritance. John's emphasis on the future, while not nearly as prominent as his stress on the present, is nevertheless sufficiently frequent to suggest that he is not rejecting such an idea from his theology. Jesus speaks of the need for the disciples to gather "fruit for eternal life" (4:36). He confirms a future resurrection (5:28–29). He promises to "prepare a place" for them and to come back to receive them to himself (14:2–3). Other passages that appear to focus on the future are the following: 4:14; 5:39; 6:27,39,40,44,54; 11:24; 12:25; 21:22; I John 2:25; 3:2; 4:17.

Some have attributed all futuristic references in John to an ecclesiastical redactor, some editor of The Gospel According to John who after the book was written is supposed to have made modifications of what was written in order to bring John into conformity with the eschatological expectations of the mainstream of the Christian church at that time. Others are convinced that the eschatology found in John was there from the beginning. Alf Correll, for example, writes:

> On the contrary, they are an organic part of Johannine theology, revealing as they do that St. John's is a true eschatology.[4]

John does not understand the contemporary experience of Christians to exhaust the meaning of the Christian doctrine of the resurrection. Men have life through the Son, but there still remains the hope of the resurrection (6:39 ff.). As C. K. Barrett aptly comments:

The problem of Johannine eschatology lies in the evangelist's firm maintenance of this essentially Christian tension, and in his use of new insights, and new terminology, in expressing it.[5]

Barrett in another place makes the further statement:

> The eschatological element in the fourth gospel is not accidental; it is fundamental. To have abandoned it would have been to abandon the biblical framework of primitive Christianity, and to run the risks to which a purely metaphysical Christianity, divorced from history, is exposed.[6]

There does not seem to be anything distinctive about John's futuristic eschatology. He does introduce a new terminology when he quotes Jesus as saying:

> In my Father's house are many rooms; if it were not so, would I have told you that I go to prepare a place for you? (14:2)

The word rendered "rooms" in the RSV means literally "abiding places" or "resting places." The word *(monē)* occurs only here and in 14:23, where Jesus promises that he and the Father will come to the believer "and make our home *(monē)* with him." The verb related to this noun, *menein,* is very prominent in the next chapter of John, where it is translated "remain" or "abide." An example would be: "Abide in me, and I in you" (15:4). The word *monē* in no way describes the nature of the place that is being prepared for the believer. It describes instead its function. Its purpose is to provide a "home," a residence, a dwelling place for the follower of God. Its chief characteristic is that it is in God's presence, that is, in his "house." Communion, fellowship, and the enjoyment of the presence of God is the uppermost thought. Because of this the rendering "mansion" (KJV) is misleading in terms of modern English usage, for it suggests a palatial residence. The translation "room" (RSV) errs on the opposite extreme, suggesting a "rooming house" or barracks, as one correspondent once wrote to me. The thought is that we enter into

God's presence in the age to come. No description of the place is implied by the word *monē*. The nature of the future life transcends experience. Therefore in I John it is written,

> It does not yet appear what we shall be, but we know that when he appears we shall be like him, for we shall see him as he is. (I John 3:2)

In general, John's distinctiveness is that he stresses Christ's presence now and that he speaks of a present resurrection to new life and a present passing from death to life (5:24). This is where he places the focus. The more traditional eschatology is not removed. It is retained, but it is overshadowed by the "realized" and "existential" character of John's message.

"Life" in the Synoptic Gospels viewed exclusively as a future inheritance. The word "life" (*zōē*) occurs only sixteen times in the Synoptic Gospels, in eight of which it is accompanied by the adjective "eternal." In two instances the word "life" (used without the adjective "eternal") simply refers to a man's existence on earth or to his life-span (Luke 12:15; 16:25). In all the other instances "life" is used in a religious sense. This particular use of "life" differs in one most important particular from the way it is used in John. In the Synoptics it is *always* viewed as a future inheritance, never as a present possession. In John it is seen as both a present possession and a future inheritance. What is unique about John is his emphasis on life as a *present reality*. This finds no parallel in the Synoptic Gospels.

Just as in John, "life" and "eternal life" are treated as synonyms in the Synoptics. They are placed parallel to each other, for example, in the following verses:

> "Teacher, what good deed must I do, to have *eternal life?*" And he said to him, . . . "If you would enter *life*, keep the commandments." (Matt. 19:16–17)

Here, and in every other instance in which life is referred to in a religious sense in the Synoptics, it has reference to a hope which the believer will realize in the age to come. The futuristic dimension of eternal life is well illustrated by the statement found in Luke:

> Truly, I say to you, there is no man who has left house or wife or brothers or parents or children, for the sake of the kingdom of God, who will not receive manifold more in this time, and *in the age to come* eternal life. (Luke 18:29–30)

By way of contrast John speaks of eternal life as a *present* possession:

> Truly, truly, I say to you, he who believes *has* eternal life. (John 6:47)

"Life" and the kingdom of God. John equates "eternal life" with "entering the kingdom of God." In ch. 3 those who believe are promised "eternal life" (3:15–16). It is in this context that the author speaks of "seeing the kingdom of God" and of "entering the kingdom of God" (3:3,5). These are but variant ways to express the same concept. They tell what opportunity lay before Nicodemus in his encounter with Jesus. This opportunity is a present one, not a future hope, according to John.

It is well to note how infrequently John refers to the kingdom of God. In fact, the above two instances are the only ones where the phrase occurs. The word *basileia* ("kingdom") by itself occurs three times in one verse (18:36; RSV, "kingship"). Except for the above references, John has completely replaced the concept of the kingdom, which occurs with great frequency in the Synoptics, with the theme of "life." The remarkable difference in the number of times the word "kingdom" occurs in the Gospels can be seen from the table on p. 42.

In one instance in the Synoptics, "life" is equated to the

	Matt.	Mark	Luke	John
basileia ("kingdom")	57	20	46	5

kingdom in its future aspect. This can be seen in the parallelism of three verses in Mark:

> And if your hand causes you to sin, cut it off; it is better for you to *enter life* maimed than with two hands to go to hell, to the unquenchable fire. (Mark 9:43)

> And if your foot causes you to sin, cut it off; it is better for you to *enter life* lame than with two feet to be thrown into hell. (Mark 9:45)

> And if your eye causes you to sin, pluck it out; it is better for you to *enter the kingdom of God* with one eye than with two eyes to be thrown into hell. (Mark 9:47)

In the first two cases, reference is made to entering into life; in the third, to entering the kingdom of God. The expressions are obviously being treated as equivalents. This equating of "life" with the "kingdom" in the Synoptic tradition indicates that John's paralleling of them in ch. 3 is not original with him. What is distinct is that the term "kingdom of God" is almost completely absent from the Fourth Gospel. "Life" has become the dominant word and has displaced the concept of the "kingdom."

The almost total disappearance of the idea of the kingdom of God in John and the preference for the expression "life" or "eternal life" led Franz Mussner[7] to suggest three reasons why this has taken place.

1. With the perception of the actual reality of the possession of life by believers the idea of the kingdom of God (which carries such an immediate eschatological coloring) was not suited for use.

2. The concept of life permitted a Christocentric emphasis

without hindrance, whereas the theocentric understanding of the kingdom within the Jewish tradition was less suitable for this.

3. The concept of life was better suited for the internalization of the gift of salvation than was the concept of the kingdom.

John's view of "life" related to his Christology. From John's perspective, the age to come became a reality in history in the ministry of Jesus. The eschatological age was qualitatively present because the Christ of the age to come was even now among men. The eschatological salvation which Judaism identified with the "age to come" had already begun. The life of the coming age had come out of the future into the present. This gave the basis for rejoicing and celebration. Since the coming of the Son, each moment in history possesses an eschatological quality.

Since Jesus is "the way, and the truth, and the life," it can properly be said that "he who has the Son has life" (I John 5:12). The crucial question to be asked, therefore, is not, When will the return of Jesus take place? but instead, How does a person appropriate for himself the life which is to be found in Christ? Mussner[8] appears to be correct in observing that John's shift from the stress on the eschatological future to the present life of the Christian is a consequence of his Christology. If Christ and eschatological salvation are identical, then this salvation is already a reality in the present time. Mussner does not view this as a totally new idea in the New Testament. He sees a connection between it and the preaching of the early church regarding "the enthronement of the Son of Man at the right hand of the Father." Mussner maintains that John has expanded and developed these ideas to a much fuller and intensive degree than is found anywhere else in the New Testament.

Two other authors draw much the same conclusion as Mussner has in tying together John's Christology and his view of salvation as a present possession. U. E. Simon writes:

> John releases the believers from a purely apocalyptic concept of life because of his interpretation of Jesus. Since Christ is the exalted Lord it would be absurd for his people merely to wait for life in Heaven.[9]

Similarly R. Schnackenburg states:

> In John . . . the strongest motive is the Christology, which shows the glory of the Logos still dwelling in the earthly Jesus, and the power of the exalted and glorified Lord already present in his word and work of salvation. In John, Christ is really the "eschatological present." [10]

Another factor that may have contributed to the shift of emphasis, and one that Schnackenburg also draws attention to, was "the recession of an imminent expectation of the end." [11] Jesus was already present with his church. "Appropriate what is yours," says the writer of the Fourth Gospel. "Don't look only to the future but enter now into the richness of the salvation which Jesus has made possible." This does not do away with the traditional view of eschatology. It shifts the emphasis, however, so that now it can be said with conviction and enthusiasm, "He that has the Son *has* life" (I John 5:12). The life which we possess through Jesus Christ is life as God intended it to be; it is "life in fullness" (10:10).

Summary of John's view of "life." Life is centered in fellowship with God. It is a present possession for believers, but it also has a future and richer fulfillment which awaits the return of Christ. Jesus is uniquely the one who has life in himself and he is the one who gives it to men. Men receive it through believing. It embodies in itself all that is meant by salvation. By "life" John means "eternal life." It is the life of the age to come already realized in the present. It is by its very nature imperishable. It is first and foremost, however, qualitatively different from mere existence. The quantitative aspect of "life," namely, that it endures forever, is a secondary motif. Regarding the demands made on those who receive life through the Son, a fine summary statement is found in R. Schnackenburg, who writes:

> The godly life granted to the Christian becomes a moral obligation: it requires a steadfastness in brotherly love. . . . The life granted by God is a life with God, which must prove true in association with people (I John 4:20 f.). Christian existence, which is spoken of under the concept of life, is a gift and a duty in one, and only in this way is its ultimate realization assured.[12]

3

~~~~~~

Jesus as the Word

The centrality of Christology. In John's statement of purpose his reason for writing is clearly related to Christology. He says,

> These are written that you may believe that Jesus is the Christ, the Son of God. (20:31)

A study of the contents of the Fourth Gospel supports the fact that the person of Jesus is the central concern of the author. Throughout the Gospel a great variety of titles are given to him. These include: the Word (*logos*), the Christ, Lord, God, Lamb of God, King of Israel, the Prophet, Rabbi, the Son, Son of Man, and Son of God. In addition to these, a large number of descriptions of Jesus are given in which he speaks of himself in the first person. These are the "I am" sayings of John. Examples would be, "I am the light of the world" (8:12; 9:5) and "I am the way, and the truth, and the life" (14:6).

Two very important observations must be made when it is said that the person of Jesus is the central concern of the author. The reason he is central is that he is presented as the link between God and man. Consequently John's Christology focuses upon both God and man.

1. Jesus came to reveal the Father. John's Christology is to be understood in the light of his theology. John is Christocentric only to a degree. He is ultimately and centrally theocentric.[1]

2. John's goal is that men may find "life." This means that his Christology is aimed at and finds ultimate meaning in soteriology.[2]

Jesus as the link between God and man finds early and dramatic expression in the Fourth Gospel. It is found, of course, in the Logos doctrine of the Prologue, but it is also implied in the indirect reference to the ladder which in Jacob's dream joined heaven and earth (Gen. 28:12). What Jacob had dreamed about had become a reality in the person of Jesus Christ. Therefore Jesus says,

> Truly, truly, I say to you, you will see heaven opened, and the angels of God ascending and descending upon the Son of man. (1:51)

"The Son of man," a messenger from heaven (cf. Dan. 7:13), has come to make God known. He has come from above to reveal the Father to men who are here below. Upon the completion of his mission he will return to the Father, who sent him into the world. The descending-ascending motif finds frequent expression in the Fourth Gospel. It is perhaps most clearly stated in the following verse:

> No one has ascended into heaven but he who descended from heaven, the Son of man. (3:13)

W. H. Cadman makes this verse a key to his understanding of the Fourth Gospel. Hence the title of his book, *The Open Heaven*. Concerning the verse, he writes that the imagery in his judgment means

> that a new intercourse between heaven and earth, between God and men, a new relation of shared life, would now set in,

on account of the divine-human person and of the whole
ministry of Jesus in uttered word, sign and Passion.[3]

In John 1:51 Jesus speaks of himself as "the Son of man."
This term is found thirteen times in the Fourth Gospel, and
because of the significance given this expression by the author
it plays a much more important role in this Gospel than does
the well-known expression "the Word," which is confined to
the Prologue and never occurs in the book after 1:14.[4]

"We have beheld his glory." In a number of ways the
manner in which the Fourth Gospel presents Jesus differs
from the picture given in the Synoptics. One of the most
dramatic differences is that The Gospel According to John
portrays for us a "glorious Christ." The author has seen
Christ's glory and he writes to share that glory with his
readers. Therefore in the Prologue he states,

> And the Word became flesh and dwelt among us, full of grace
> and truth; we have beheld his glory, glory as of the only Son
> from the Father. (1:14)

While John 1:14 has often been cited as stressing the full
humanity of Jesus through the words, "And the Word
became *flesh,*" E. Käsemann maintains that this is not the key
idea of the passage. The main thought comes later in the
verse where the stress is on Jesus' *glory* and on the fact that in
and through him the Father is revealed among men. Käsemann writes:

> The "presence of God" on earth is the real goal of the
> becoming flesh. . . . His becoming flesh is the manifestation
> of the Creator on earth. . . . Incarnation for John is really
> epiphany.[5]

E. C. Colwell and E. L. Titus have drawn attention to the
fact that the portrayal of Jesus throughout the Fourth Gospel
highlights his divine majesty. Concerning Jesus they write:

> He walks upon the stage in the first scene of this Gospel clad
> in the full panoply of divinity and moves majestically and

irresistibly through the program on which he and his divine Father have agreed. . . . All Jesus' actions and all his words are manifestations of the divine glory which the Father bestowed upon him before Abraham's day.[6]

Because of this consistent aura of majesty which surrounds Jesus in the Fourth Gospel and because of the stress in John on the preexistence of "the Son," it appears to be valid to say that in this Gospel there is an advance or development in Christology which goes beyond that expressed in the Synoptic Gospels. Christ's glory is constantly being manifested. This may be one reason why in the Fourth Gospel there is no transfiguration scene comparable to that found in the Synoptics. There was no need for such a portrayal of the majesty of Jesus in John since every miracle he performed and even his trial and passion manifested his glory to men.

So early is Jesus' identity known in this Gospel that in the very first chapter he is confessed by those who meet him with almost every title used in the Christology of the early church. There is no hidden messiahship comparable to that found in the Synoptics where Peter's confession does not come until halfway through the Gospel accounts and more than halfway through Jesus' public ministry. In fact, in the last chapter of Luke the disciples on the road to Emmaus are still not sure whether Jesus was the Messiah or not (Luke 24:21).

Christ's arrest can come only when he allows it. All this happens only when "his hour" has come. This hour is determined by God's timetable, not by man's. Pilate has no power over him apart from the Father's permissive will. The scene of Jesus' trial results in the condemnation of Pilate rather than of Jesus, for Jesus, as "the truth," stands before Pilate and Pilate fails to recognize or acknowledge the truth. Jesus' death on the cross is not a tragic end to a heroic life. It is the glorious consummation of the eternal plan of God. It is therefore in John's Gospel (and only in John's) that Jesus utters the cry of victory from the cross: "It is finished"

(19:30). Jesus is referring not to the end of his life but to the successful completion of his mission. These are words of triumph, not defeat: *Tetelestai* (Greek); *Consummatum est* (Vulgate); "It is accomplished!" (NEB).

Jesus as the Logos. The earliest title given to Jesus in The Gospel According to John is "the Word" (*ho logos,* 1:1). The introduction to this Gospel is quite different from the introductions found in the Gospels of Matthew, Mark, and Luke. Mark, which is probably the earliest of the Gospels, begins with an account of Jesus' baptism. Matthew and Luke begin with the story of Jesus' birth in Bethlehem. Matthew, who seems to be writing primarily for those who are well acquainted with the Old Testament, traces the ancestry of Jesus back to Abraham, the father of the Hebrew nation (Matt. 1:1). Luke, who writes primarily for readers of Gentile origin, traces Jesus' ancestry back even farther, for he speaks of him as descended from Adam, who was created by God (Luke 3:38). Adam was viewed as the father of the whole human race. Whereas Matthew identifies Jesus especially with the Jews, Luke relates him to all of humanity. One might think that Luke has gone back as far as it is possible to go. But, no! John takes his readers back even farther than Adam and relates the Word to the act of creation itself. Even before creation, that is, "in the beginning," the Word existed. John by his creative and dramatic imagery takes us back to the place where the ocean of eternity thunders on the shores of time. "In the beginning," says John, "was the Word." Patterned after Gen. 1:1, the opening of John's Gospel ties "the Word" to God's creation of the universe.

In addition to relating "the Word" to creation, John enriches this descriptive term by having it express his doctrines of incarnation and revelation. The former of these finds expression in the words, "And the Word became flesh and dwelt among us" (1:14). The latter idea, that of revelation (or manifestation), is embraced in the phrase, "We have beheld his glory, glory as of the only Son from the Father" (1:14). For centuries men had sought to understand the nature of the divine, to unravel the mysteries of an invisible God. Now He who was invisible has made himself visible. The One who dwelt in transcendent glory in the heavens has deigned to dwell (literally, "he pitched his tent," *eskēnōsen*) among us (1:14).

The Prologue is not so much an introduction to The Gospel According to John as it is a summation of its thought and theology. Here in brief compass and in phrasing that combines simplicity with dignity we have the essence of the Johannine message. God has revealed his glory and himself in the person of the Son, Jesus of Nazareth. This identification of the Word with Jesus is not made until v. 17 of the Prologue.

Identifying Jesus with the term *logos,* "the Word," is unique to Johannine literature. Outside The Gospel According to John, Logos as a title is used only in I John 1:1 and in Rev. 19:13. It occurs nowhere else in the New Testament. In the Gospel of John it is confined to the Prologue. While it is a distinctly Johannine term, "the Word" is not John's most important title for Jesus or the one that he feels best expresses his Christology.

The term Logos did not originate with John. It was used earlier in Greek literature by Stoic philosophers who meant by it the rational structure of the universe. Philo, a Jewish philosopher who died about A.D. 50, used it frequently in his efforts to bridge Greek and Hebrew thought. Philo appears to have been deeply influenced by Stoic philosophy. Oscar Cullmann writes,

Although Philo's Logos doctrine lacks unity and has various roots, the Stoic conception of the Logos as the principle of reason in the world prevails in his writings.[7]

No direct line can be drawn from Philo to the Prologue. As H. Conzelmann observes,

> The Johannine Logos has nothing to do with an understanding of the world in terms of reason.[8]

Some sought to find the origin of Logos in Gnosticism. Rudolf Bultmann has written,

> The mythological figure of the Logos has its home in a particular understanding of the world, namely, the Gnostic.[9]

This view is not the prevailing one at the present time. Joachim Jeremias[10] argues that the Logos presentation is generally strange to the Gnostic system and where it does occur it is derived from John's Prologue. The tendency today is to find the spring for John's Logos doctrine in Jewish Wisdom literature.[11] As C. H. Dodd has written:

> In composing the Prologue the author's mind was moving along lines similar to those followed by Jewish writers of the "Wisdom" school.[12]

In the Old Testament and in other writings of Hellenistic Judaism a genre of literature emerged which came to be known as Wisdom Literature. In this material, Wisdom was personified. Wisdom speaks, for example, and says,

> I, wisdom, dwell in prudence,
> and I find knowledge and discretion.
> (Prov. 8:12)

Wisdom is described as being God's agent in the creation of the world:

> When he marked out the foundations of the earth,
> then I was beside him, like a master workman.
> (Prov. 8:29–30)

Wisdom's participation in creation is said to have taken place "in the beginning" (*en archē*, Prov. 8:23), or "from the beginning" (*ap' archēs,* Sirach 24:9). In these passages Wisdom is itself created by God before it participates in the creation of the world. John does not portray the Logos as being created. He says, "In the beginning *was* the Word," thereby implying the eternal being of the Logos. This is a distinct advance beyond the Hellenistic personification of Wisdom. Furthermore, for John the Word is personal and becomes incarnate, being identified with Jesus of Nazareth. Wisdom, while personified, remains an abstract concept. It is present in the world, but it is never identified with humanity through an act of incarnation.

The terminology by which Wisdom's presence in the world is described seems to have influenced John's description of the Word's incarnation. Concerning Wisdom, it is said,

> and the one who created me
> assigned a place for my tent *(tēn skēnēn mou).*
> And he said, "Make your dwelling in Jacob" *(kataskēnōson).*
>
> (Sirach 24:8)

In describing the Word's presence in the world, John also uses the concept of "pitching one's tent." He writes that the Word "dwelt among us" (*eskēnōsen en hēmīn,* 1:14). Literally this means "to live," "to dwell," or "to take up residence." It carries the connotation that this is a temporary residence. The Word came for a short time, but then he returned to the place from which he came. This return occurred only after he had completed the purpose for which he had come.

Wisdom is spoken of as "alone in kind" (*monogenēs,* Wisd. of Sol. 7:22), a word that John uses of the Logos in 1:14 and later of Jesus in 1:18; 3:16, 18. Wisdom is also called "a pure emanation of the glory (*doxa*) of the Almighty" (Wisd. of Sol. 7:25). This expression of "glory" is associated in the Fourth Gospel with Jesus' ministry and specifically in the Prologue with the Logos when it became flesh. The author writes,

> We have beheld his glory, glory as of the only Son from the Father. (1:14)

Wisdom is compared to "light" (Wisd. of Sol. 7:29), as is the
Logos (John 1:4, 5). God is said to have made "all things" by
his "word" (Wisd. of Sol. 9:1), a phrase that closely parallels
John's phrase, "All things were made through him" (1:3).
The thought of Wisdom being active in creation is expressed
also in Prov. 3:19: "The Lord by wisdom founded the earth."
It is clear that John's Logos doctrine bears several striking
resemblances to Wisdom. The ideas he expresses are, at least
in part, at home in this milieu. At the same time, John has
gone beyond what was ever said of Wisdom. His distinctive
contribution is that he affirms that the Word was God, that it
became incarnate, and that the Word is "the only Son,"
whom the author identifies with Jesus Christ (1:1, 14, 17).

Why does John choose Logos instead of Wisdom? *Sophia*
("wisdom") is a feminine noun. *Logos,* a masculine noun, is
more appropriate to express the coming of the Son into the
world. Furthermore, Logos was current in the religious
vocabulary of his day. It provided a point of contact,
especially with John's Gentile readers. While he borrows a
currently popular religious term, he molds it to his own
purpose by having it express his own distinctive Christology.
What John meant by the Logos cannot be determined by
reading the writings of the Stoics and of Philo. That question
can be settled only by a careful exegesis of the Prologue and
by relating this to the overall Christology of the Fourth
Gospel. An observation by T. E. Pollard seems especially
valid at this point. He writes concerning the use of Logos by
the author of the Fourth Gospel:

> That he uses it primarily—we may almost say solely—as a
> point of contact should be evident from the fact that, having
> used the concept in the Prologue, he does not use it again, and
> that in his closing words he says that the purpose of his
> Gospel is "that you may believe that Jesus is the Christ, the
> Son of God, and that believing you may have life in his name"
> (20:31). The regulative christological concept of the Gospel is
> not *Logos,* but *the Christ, the Son of God.*[13]

Raymond E. Brown draws additional parallels between Logos and Wisdom and concludes:

> The Wisdom Literature offers better parallels for the Johannine picture of Jesus than do the later Gnostic, Mandean, or Hermetic passages sometimes suggested. . . . In the O.T. presentation of Wisdom, there are good parallels for almost every detail of the Prologue's description of the Word.[14]

Hypostatization of "the Word" in Judaism. In several recent studies it has been pointed out that in Judaism hypostatization of several prominent terms in addition to Wisdom developed. These researches are carefully summarized by Jack T. Sanders.[15] Lorenz Durr, for example, sees the Hebrew word *dabar* ("word") go through a process of hypostatization parallel to the development of Wisdom.[16] Sanders then goes on to relate how the study of Helmer Ringgren developed the thought of Durr and placed "this process of hypostatization in its larger context." [17] Ringgren[18] relates the process of hypostatization to the surrounding nations, Egypt and ancient Sumer and Akkad. Ringgren agrees with Durr that even in the Old Testament there is a true hypostasis of the Word. He quotes with approval Durr's conclusion that

> We find as the final stage of the development, as early as in the O.T., the divine word, emanating from the divinity, but acting independently, quietly and surely going its way, a part of the divinity, as bearer of divine power, obviously separate from God and yet belonging to him, a hypostasis in the proper sense of the word.[19]

As a result of the studies of Durr and Ringgren the conclusion is reached by Jack T. Sanders that

> the progressive hypostatization of the Word in Judaism, constantly under influence from foreign religions, comes close enough to what is said of the Logos in the Prologue of John that the prologue may be seen as merely the next stage in this process.[20]

John's greatest modification, of course, would be his affirmation that "the Word became flesh and dwelt among us." For this proclamation concerning the Logos he is not indebted to the Old Testament, to Wisdom literature, to Greek philosophy, or to the writings of Philo. This emerged from the *kerygma* of the early church which in turn found its roots in the experience of the earliest disciples with Jesus of Nazareth.

Does the Prologue incorporate an early hymn? J. Rendel Harris[21] years ago suggested that the Prologue to the Gospel of John incorporated an earlier hymn dedicated to Wisdom. Bultmann[22] sought to relate the suggested hymn to the John the Baptist movement. It was, in his opinion, a pre-Christian hymn used in this community to honor John the Baptist. R. Schnackenburg[23] presents the theory that this was a "Christian hymn" whose theology and outlook were close to the views of the writer of the Fourth Gospel and that the writer took this poem, once an independent entity, and made it the opening of his Gospel.

Käsemann's views are close to those of Schnackenburg and he questions Bultmann's suggestion that the hymn was pre-Christian. He writes:

> The pre-Christian character of the hymn is more than problematical, the Aramaic original incredible, the alleged Baptist hymn a pure hypothesis.[24]

Some remain unconvinced that John here takes over an earlier poem or hymn and prefer to regard this prologue as a balanced and rhythmic introduction especially prepared by the writer as a fitting opening to his Gospel. C. K. Barrett writes:

> The Prologue, then, stands before us as a prose introduction which has not been submitted to interpolation and was specially written (it must be supposed) to introduce the gospel.[25]

So also Robert M. Grant states that it is not necessary to project an early hymn as lying behind the Prologue. He concludes:

> Such an inference is not necessary. He may well have composed the prologue specifically for use in the gospel.[26]

While the tendency today seems to be predominantly an acceptance of the hypothesis that an earlier hymn was incorporated, there are some factors that make the views of Barrett and Grant worth considering:

1. The opening of the Prologue appears to be modeled after Gen., ch. 1. Could not this be deliberate on the part of the writer, who constantly relates Jesus to the Old Testament?

2. The Prologue is saturated with Johannine vocabulary. Non-Johannine vocabulary is minimal.

3. The so-called poetry of the Prologue does not differ markedly from the poetic prose that characterizes much of the rest of the Gospel where rhythm, balanced phrasing, and synthetical and antithetical parallelism are not infrequent.

Clearly the main ideas of the Prologue are quite congenial to John's thought. If there was an original hymn that has been incorporated, it would appear that it was not imported from some alien source. The compatibility of the main ideas of the Prologue with the content of the Fourth Gospel as a whole suggests that if a hymn was absorbed, then the hymn itself probably emerged within the circle of believers where Johannine thought was prevalent.

4

~~~~~~

Other Titles
for Jesus

The Son of Man. Thirteen times in the Fourth Gospel Jesus speaks of himself as "the Son of man." Twelve of these are in the Book of Signs (1:51; 3:13,14; 5:27; 6:27,53,62; 8:28; 9:35; 12:23,34 (twice)), and only one is in the Book of the Passion (13:31). John's use of this title leads Cullmann to comment,

> One cannot deny that the Son of Man concept is much more important than that of the Logos in the Gospel of John as a whole.[1]

In the Synoptic Gospels the Son of Man sayings have generally been divided into three types:

1. Those which speak of the present work on earth of the Son of Man.

2. Predictions of Jesus' sufferings and death.

3. Predictions of Jesus as the apocalyptic judge.

One of the most important passages in John in which the title Son of Man is used is the first one, which reads:

> Truly, truly, I say to you, you will see heaven opened, and the angels of God ascending and descending upon the Son of man. (1:51)

Through the Son of Man the heavens have been opened! He is a ladder between God the Father and mankind. He is the link, or mediator, between God and man. He has come to reveal the Father. As Käsemann has written:

> The Son of Man is . . . God, descending into the human realm and there manifesting his glory.[2]

A. J. B. Higgins[3] finds in John's use of the Son of Man title two distinctive contributions:

1. Preexistent glory is attached to the Son of Man. This is implied in 3:13 and 6:62, where stress is laid on the fact that the Son of Man has descended into the world from the presence of God.

2. In the Synoptic Gospels it is only after his death on the cross that Jesus is viewed as glorified and is envisioned as the apocalyptic judge. Glorification is associated with the resurrection and the ascension, and the designation of Jesus as judge is related to his *parousia* and the consummation of the age. In John, Jesus' glory is seen throughout his ministry but especially in his crucifixion which is spoken of as his "exaltation," or "lifting up." Jesus dies in obedience to the Father. No man takes his life from him. He lays it down and takes it up again. By such obedience both the Father and Jesus are glorified. It is also the supreme manifestation of the eternal love of God for the world.

The fact that the Son of Man is totally submitted to the will of God the Father is expressed by Jesus in the statement:

> When you have lifted up the Son of man, then you will know that I am he, and that I do nothing on my own authority but speak thus as the Father taught me. (8:28)

The Son of Man is God's messenger. His will is to do the Father's will. Käsemann captures this element well in his statement:

> For John obedience is the mark of the Son of Man who not only participates in the mission of God, but also fulfils it.[4]

How does he fulfill God's will? By giving *Life* to the world!

> And as Moses lifted up the serpent in the wilderness, so must
> the Son of man be lifted up, that whoever believes in him may
> have eternal life. (3:14–15)

The Son of Man gives eternal life (6:27,54). By dying, he
"bears much fruit" (12:23–24). In summary R. Schnackenburg writes:

> All thirteen texts in John which speak of the Son of Man form
> a consistent and well-knit whole. The Son of Man is the
> Johannine Messiah, the giver of life and judge.[5]

The reason these two opposite functions can both be true
simultaneously is that when the offer of life in Jesus is refused
by that very rejection men judge themselves. By refusing to
believe, they show themselves to be blind and they walk in
darkness. As J. Louis Martyn writes:

> The traditional motif of the Son of Man as judge, so
> prominent in 5:27, is directly acted out in 9:35–41.[6]

W. H. Cadman comments:

> The life-giver is transformed into the judge by all to whom He
> comes ineffectively.[7]

In The Gospel According to John, in other words, the
understanding of Jesus as judge is moved from the future to
the present (5:27).

The Son of God. In The Gospel According to John, Jesus is
nine times referred to as "the Son of God" (1:34, 49; 3:18;
5:25; 10:36; 11:4, 27; 19:7; 20:31). More commonly he is
simply called "the Son." This expression occurs nineteen
times in John (1:18; 3:16, 17, 35, 36 (twice); 5:19 (twice);
5:20, 21, 22, 23 (twice); 5:26; 6:40; 8:36; 14:13; 17:1 (twice)).
In seventeen of these instances the term "the Son" stands in
juxtaposition to "the Father." In two instances it stands in
juxtaposition to "God" (3:16, 17).

The author of the Fourth Gospel gives special prominence to the expression "the Son of God" by including it specifically in his statement of purpose when he writes:

These are written that you may believe that Jesus is the Christ, the Son of God, and that believing you may have life in his name. (20:31)

Some have argued that the expressions "the Son," "the Son of man," and "the Son of God" should all be equated in the Fourth Gospel.[8] A study of John 3:13–18 will indicate that all three expressions occur here in a manner which suggests that they are being used as equivalents. This does not mean, however, that certain distinct nuances are not on other occasions attached to the titles Son of Man and Son of God.

It seems clear that John uses the expressions "the Son" and "the Son of God" indiscriminately.[9] They are for the author interchangeable. When he uses the term "the Son" the correlative is immediately stated. As noted above, this is generally "the Father," but twice "God."

A study of the passages that use the expressions "the Son" or "the Son of God" appears to place special stress on the relationship that exists between Jesus and the Father. This is either a relationship of obedience or of oneness.[10] The obedience motif emerges in a passage such as the following:

Truly, truly, I say to you, the Son can do nothing of his own accord, but only what he sees the Father doing; for whatever he does, that the Son does likewise. (5:19)

The stress on oneness which finds expression in terms of love and fellowship is spoken of as follows:

The Father loves the Son, and has given all things into his hand. (3:35)

This title is viewed by John as containing the essence of the Christian confession. It is the confession of this belief that separates those who believe from those who do not. It is because Jesus claimed to be "the Son of God" that the authorities are said to have sought his death (10:36; 19:7). For Jesus to call himself "the Son of God" was equivalent to claiming to be God himself (10:33). The expression "the Son of God" is then an acknowledgment of Jesus' deity. It would be equivalent to the affirmation of the Prologue, "And the Word was God" in 1:14 and to Thomas' confession, "My Lord and my God!" (20:28). Confessing Jesus to be "the Son of man" can also imply saving faith, as in 9:35 ff. This suggests that there is a definite overlapping of meaning between the titles Son of Man and Son of God. If any distinction can be made between "Son of Man" and "Son of God," perhaps it is in the fact that the former puts an emphasis upon the descent and ascent of the preexistent Son of Man who is the mediator between God and man. "The Son of God" as a title (or "the Son") puts special stress on the person of the Son and on his unique relationship with the Father. That he is the "unique" *(monogenēs)* Son occurs only in phrases tying "unique" to the Father (1:14), or to "the Son" (1:18; although here the better reading may be *monogenēs theos,* "only-begotten or unique God," and 3:16), or to "the Son of God." This adjective *(monogenēs)* does not occur with the Son of Man. E. Schweizer concludes that in John

> the title Son of God has already become a cipher which presupposes a unity of essence between Father and Son without defining it more precisely.[11]

To confess Jesus as "the Son of God" is the mark of a believer (1:34; 3:18). This title is also considered normative in I John 4:15 and 5:5.

J. Coutts agrees that "the Son of God" is the central confession of the Fourth Gospel. He writes:

> For both Mark and John the supreme title of Jesus is Son of God, and under this other titles are to be subsumed. Both

emphasize, though John much more richly, that this is not properly a Messianic title but a description of the intimate relationship of Father and Son.[12]

In John, more than in any other New Testament writing, the Sonship of Jesus is the central motif. As W. F. Lofthouse has put it:

> In John Christ is primarily and pre-eminently the Son of the Father. From this relationship spring all the various functions of Christ. It is because He is the Son, and holds this unique relation to the Father, that He is the source of all our blessings.[13]

Except for the rather unusual use of "the Son of man" in 9:35 f., this title is not a confessional formula. Perhaps the fact that textual variants arose in which "the Son of God" is substituted indicates that others sensed that the latter term is the more normal one used in confessing faith in Jesus. Furthermore, as in the case of the Synoptics, only Jesus uses "Son of man" as a self-designation. He is never so addressed by others.

God's only Son. The expression "the Son" is characteristic of the Johannine writings. While it occurs three times in the Synoptics (Matt. 11.27, parallel Luke 10:22; Mark 13:32, parallel Matt. 24:36; and Matt. 28:19), once in Paul (I Cor. 15:28), and five times in Hebrews, once without the article (Heb. 1:2, 8; 3:6; 5:8; 7:28), in John it occurs eighteen times (possibly nineteen if 1:18 is included) plus five times in I John and once in II John. It is also implied by the many times when Jesus speaks of God as "the Father." This leads Schnackenburg to conclude that " 'The Father-Son Relationship' is the key to the understanding of the Johannine Jesus." [14] He writes:

> Jesus is the revelation, the portrayal, the Word in the world of the invisible and for men the inaccessible God. Everything

that he said and proclaimed on earth, occurs at the behest of
God, in order to mediate salvation, namely, eternal life, to
men.[15]

This idea is well expressed also by G. Schrenk, who wrote:

The Father is the author and giver of revelation, the Son is the
Revealer. . . . The whole event of salvation is anchored in the
most intimate union between Father and Son.[16]

The uniqueness of Jesus' relationship to the Father is
occasionally expressed in John by the adjective *monogenēs,*
meaning "only." This word occurs in 1:14, 18; 3:16, 18. The
word means basically "single of its kind, only." [17] This word

is used in the Septuagint to translate the Hebrew word yachid
(cf. Amos 8:10; Zech. 12:10), which has the literal meaning of
"dear one" or "one and only." [18]

In the Wisdom of Solomon 7:22 this adjective is applied to
Wisdom. F. Büchsel makes the comment,

One should not refer the *monogenes* to the virgin birth of
Jesus, for the pre-existent as well as the historical Jesus is the
Son of God.[19]

Leon Morris writes:

Jesus is God's Son in a unique way. No other can be the Son
of God as He is. The unique character of the relationship
between the Father and the Son is one of the great themes of
this Gospel.[20]

As the Son, Jesus both *(a)* reveals the Father, since he has
a unique relationship to him which implies unique knowledge, and *(b)* is subordinate to the Father. Both elements are
present in the Fourth Gospel.[21] John's Christology always
stresses that the Son is the one sent by the Father to do the
Father's will and to reveal the Father to men. Hence, as
noted earlier, epiphany and soteriology are for John the
ultimate goals of the incarnation of the Son.

The "I am" sayings. The "I am" formulas of the Fourth Gospel are a distinctive characteristic. They fall into two categories: (1) those used absolutely, and (2) those followed by a predicate. Jesus speaks the words "I am" absolutely in the following passages: 4:26; 6:20; 8:24, 28, 58; 13:19; 18:5, 6, 8. Jesus uses "I am" with a predicate in these verses: 6:35, 41, 48, 51; 8:12, 18; 10:7, 9, 11, 14; 11:25; 14:6; 15:1, 5. To these should probably be added 8:23, where Jesus says, "I am from above; . . . I am not of this world."

The Synoptic Gospels never present Jesus as using the "I am" statement with an expressed predicate, with the possible exception of Matt. 24:5, where in the Olivet discourse Jesus predicts that others will come after him and say "I am the Christ." This manner of speaking, then, is distinctively and exclusively Johannine. The direct "I am" statements of John (especially those with the predicate) are a different presentation of Jesus than that found in the Synoptics, where the messianic secret is such a pervasive theme. In John, Jesus repeatedly makes great personal claims through this formula. In the Synoptics the note of authority is also present in the teachings of Jesus, but it is not expressed by this particular terminology. It finds expression instead when Jesus says,

> Every one then who hears these words of mine and does them will be like a wise man who built his house upon the rock. (Matt. 7:24)

The writer then concludes,

> The crowds were astonished at his teaching, for he taught them as one who had authority, and not as their scribes. (Matt. 7:28–29)

The authority is focused on the teaching of Jesus. This, of course, carries implications as to who Jesus is. What is *implied* in the Synoptics is stated openly by Jesus in the Johannine discourses. There the matter of the person of

Jesus is not left to inference. In the "I am" sayings Jesus bears clear and repeated witness to himself.

There are seven major "I am" affirmations made by Jesus in which he uses some image (generally derived from Old Testament symbolism) to declare who he is. These are:

1. "I am the bread of life (living bread)" (6:35,41,51).
2. "I am the light of the world" (8:12; (9:5 with *egō* omitted)).
3. "I am the door" (10:7,9).
4. "I am the good shepherd" (10:11,14).
5. "I am the resurrection and the life" (11:25).
6. "I am the way, and the truth, and the life" (14:6).
7. "I am the true vine" (15:1,5).

Egō eimi used absolutely. In John 8:58, Jesus says, "Truly, truly, I say to you, before Abraham was, I am." W. Manson commented on this verse:

> There is an intentional contraposition of "existence" and "becoming" . . . which shows that *Ego eimi* is the claim to an existence above history and time. . . . The Jesus of the Fourth Gospel is the Eternal Logos who, as such, shares and manifests to men the life of God.[22]

In John 13:19 there appears to be the same absolute use of the expression "I am." The RSV translation supplies the word "he," but this is not in the Greek. The verse in the RSV reads,

> I·tell you this now, before it takes place, that when it does take place you may believe that I am he.

The NEB, recognizing that the expression "I am" is reminiscent of Old Testament usage for the divine name, translates this verse as follows:

> I tell you this now, before the event, that when it happens you may believe that I am what I am.

Here the translators are clearly allowing their rendering to be determined by Ex. 3:14, where God says to Moses, "I AM WHO I AM" or "I AM WHAT I AM." The Greek in John 13:19 has only the words *egō eimi*. It would be appropriate, therefore, to render 13:19 in the same way that the RSV rendered 8:58. It would then read:

I tell you this now, before it takes place, that when it does take place you may believe that I am.

Philip B. Harner, in a recent study, has come to the conclusion that Deutero-Isaiah rather than Exodus is the most significant influence behind the "I am" sayings of the Fourth Gospel. He writes:

The I AM of Exodus 3:14 can hardly be considered a direct source for Johannine usage. At most it is indirectly related to the Fourth Gospel in the sense that it may have influenced the Septuagint translators in their rendering of *'ani hu* in Second Isaiah as *egō eimi*. Our examination of the absolute *egō eimi* in the Fourth Gospel confirms this view, for we have not found any specific aspects of the phrase that would be especially reminiscent of Exodus 3:14.[23]

In Deutero-Isaiah, God is repeatedly spoken of as *egō eimi* in the Septuagint rendering of the Hebrew words *'ani hu'*, meaning literally "I am He" (Isa. 41:4; 43:10,13,25) There is considerable agreement today that John's absolute use of "I am" finds its closest parallel in Deutero-Isaiah.[24] John 10:38 bears a close similarity to Isa. 43:10:

But if I do them, even though you do not believe me, believe the works, that you may know and understand that the Father is in me and I am in the Father. (John 10:38)

"You are my witnesses," says the Lord,
"and my servant whom I have chosen,
that you may know and believe me
and understand that I am He."
(Isa. 43:10)

The verbs "believe" and "know" are identical in John and in the Septuagint rendering of Isaiah. For "understand" the verbs differ in the Greek but are synonyms. The closeness of phrasing suggests that the author has been influenced by the kind of phrasing found in Deutero-Isaiah.

Harner[25] comments that there is nothing in the Hellenistic religious milieu which parallels the absolute use of "I am" as found in John and that therefore one cannot claim this literature as a source for this expression. Similarly R. Schnackenburg after citing Old Testament parallels to the absolute "I am" statements of John states concerning the latter:

> When these passages show such a clear reflection of the Old Testament revelation formula and when for this absolute manner of discourse (without more detailed qualification or explanation through a symbol) no other parallels are to be found, the influence of the Old Testament upon them is certainly assured.[26]

The "I am" sayings used with a predicate. When John expands the absolute "I am" sayings, however, a form of expression results which has no exact parallel in the Old Testament, including Deutero-Isaiah. This led R. Bultmann[27] to posit proto-Mandaean influence on John, and E. Schweizer[28] to suggest that John and the Mandaean writings shared a common source. H. Zimmermann[29] argues that an appeal to Mandaean influence is unnecessary to explain John's "I am" formulas when they are used with various images. The various images simply express what Jesus has to give to men—namely, bread, light, life, truth, etc. He not only gives these but *is* for men the bread of life and so forth. This is just a further step in the development of the revelation formula. A. Feuillet,[30] on the other hand, takes the position that these "I am" statements go back to Jesus himself and that they reflect his own awareness of who he was and that they reveal this to men even though his hearers do not fully understand what is meant by these sayings until later. Others would agree with Zimmermann in attributing these developed formulations to later Christian reflection rather than to Jesus himself. Harner writes,

> The *ego eimi* represents an attempt to formulate and express the significance of Jesus in Christian faith.[31]

Barnabas Lindars similarly concludes:

> The "I am" sayings . . . are the *consequences* of his Christology. It is because John *arrives at* a Wisdom Christology in his attempt to expound Jesus' origins, that he uses this formula from time to time to express the gift of Jesus in terms of a Wisdom invitation.[32]

R. Schnackenburg attributes the absolute use of "I am" to the influence of the Deutero-Isaiah formula. The revelation formula of Yahweh has been transferred to Jesus. Furthermore, the content of the symbolism found in the "I am" sayings when they are not used absolutely is also derived from Old Testament and Judaical roots. The form, however, since it has no parallel in the Old Testament has probably been influenced by "the soteriological style of discourse found in eastern Hellenism." [33] He suggests that even in the case of the choice of imagery the possibility that there has been some influence from this source cannot be excluded. He argues for this in the light of the fact that the Gospel of John may be viewed as building a bridge from the Biblical-Jewish sphere to the Hellenistic world. He writes,

> Such a process is very conceivable for an evangelist (or a theological school) who does not deny his origin in Judaism, but who is also open to the syncretistic world about him.[34]

Jesus and the "I am" sayings. Schnackenburg would not regard these "I am" sayings in their expanded form as going back directly to Jesus. He writes:

> It is . . . clear that the Johannine *ego eimi* discourses stand
> totally in the service of Johannine Christology and the
> doctrine of salvation. They are a distinctive formulation
> alongside of other expressions of Johannine Christology (the
> Son, the Son of Man, the Lamb of God), which commends
> itself especially in that it makes clear, through striking images
> and symbols, the salvation character of the sending of Jesus.[35]

The various symbols used are but variations of the theme that
Jesus has come into the world in order that men may have life
and have it in all its fullness (10:10). The "I am" sayings
emerged in the instruction of the church and in its missionary
outreach, as it sought to express who Jesus is and why he
came into the world.

E. Stauffer is convinced that at least some of the "I am"
sayings go back to Jesus himself. He writes:

> There can . . . be no doubt that these theophanic formulae
> had their source in Jesus himself. We cannot say that Jesus
> actually spoke all the theophanic sayings attributed to him by
> our various witnesses, that he spoke only these, or that he
> spoke them in exactly the situations and using exactly the
> words reported. But we can with confidence maintain that the
> theophanic formula *"Ani hu"* was of crucial importance in
> Jesus' revelation of himself.[36]

By this expression, says Stauffer, Jesus "wished to convey that
in his life the historical epiphany of God was taking place." [37]

Raymond E. Brown draws attention to the fact that when
Jesus walks on the water and is seen by the disciples from the
boat he answers in both Mark and John, *"Egō eimi"* (Mark
6:50; John 6:20). He also draws attention to some other
places in the Synoptics where the absolute use of the words "I
am" appears to reflect the revelation formula, namely, Mark
14:62 (Luke 22:70), Luke 24:39, and a reference to false
claims by others who will come in Jesus' name in Mark 13:6
(Luke 21:8). He concludes:

Thus, John's absolute use of "I am" . . . may be an elaboration of a use of "I am" attributed to Jesus in the Synoptic tradition as well. Once again, rather than creating from nothing, Johannine theology may have capitalized on a valid theme of the early tradition.[38]

Through the "I am" sayings when used with a predicate we are presented confessions of faith by the early church. These affirmations of faith express what the Christians found Jesus to be. The "I am" sayings are "true" because they give a valid interpretation of the person and meaning of Jesus even though they apparently go beyond verbal reporting of the actual words that Jesus himself used.

5

~~~~~~

The Children of God

The Gospel of John consistently presupposes a gathered Christian community. To this community the author gives encouragement, instruction, exhortation, and admonition. Its presence is not only constantly implied but celebrated. Positive hopes and expectations are expressed about this company of believers, for it is the author's conviction that to this fellowship has been given not only the revelation of God but also the mandate to share that revelation with the world. In the view of the writer the focus of history centers on this closely knit band of disciples of Jesus and on their followers, those, namely, who have responded to their witness.

Although the word "church" never occurs in the Gospel of John, the church is nevertheless a very prominent theme. The idea of the church is presented in a wide variety of images and expressions.

IMAGES OF THE CHURCH

The bride and the bridegroom. The imagery of the bride as representing the church is found in Eph. 5:21–33 and in Rev.

72

21:2. It is also found in the Fourth Gospel. It is implied in the statement of John the Baptist in his relationship to Jesus. He says:

> He who has the bride is the bridegroom; the friend of the bridegroom, who stands and hears him, rejoices greatly at the bridegroom's voice; therefore this joy of mine is now full. (3:29)

The children of God. A designation that is introduced early in the Gospel and repeated in fuller form in ch. 11 is the phrase "the children of God" *(ta tekna tou theou).* This phrase seems to be normative for the author's understanding of the church.[1] The passages in which it is found read as follows:

> But to all who received him, who believed in his name, he gave power to become *children of God.* (1:12)

> But one of them, Caiaphas, who was high priest that year, said to them, "You know nothing at all; you do not understand that it is expedient for you that one man should die for the people, and that the whole nation should not perish." He did not say this of his own accord, but being high priest that year he prophesied that Jesus should die for the nation, and not for the nation only, but to gather into one the *children of God* who are scattered abroad. (11:49–52)

It is not the frequency of use which makes this phrase stand out in the Gospel of John (although this designation is found in a number of very significant passages in I John, e.g., 3:1,2,10; 5:2) but the degree to which this expression captures and expresses within itself the heart of the Johannine teaching concerning the church.

The designation "the children of God" appears to carry with it two major connotations in Johannine theology:

1. It speaks first of the filial relationship (i.e., sonship) which is established between the believer and God. The

believer has been "born of God" (1:13), "born from above" (3:3), and "born of the Spirit" (3:8). These are variant ways of expressing the same basic truth, namely, that he now belongs to God and that God dwells in him (14:23).

2. The second meaning of the phrase "the children of God" derives from Semitic usage, where the expression "son of" or "child of" is normally descriptive of character. It tells something about the person, what he is like, what he does, or where his allegiance is. This can be illustrated from a few examples from both the Old and the New Testament. In Deut. 13:13 we are told about certain persons who are called "children of Belial" (KJV). Literally "Belial" means "worthless," "useless." Recent translations give the meaning more clearly when they call these persons "base fellows" (RSV) and "miscreants" (NEB). Examples from the New Testament would be "sons of thunder" (Mark 3:17) and "children of the devil" (I John 3:10).

When believers are called "the children of God," therefore, the expression carries the connotation that they are persons who both belong to God and are concerned to do the will of God. The designation is a qualitative phrase that is descriptive of their inner life, of their new allegiance, and of their new sense of values. They have acknowledged the sovereignty of God over their lives. As "the children of God," they pursue God's ways among men and are as "light" in the midst of "darkness." Consequently they can appropriately be given the corollary designation "sons of light" *(huioi phōtos,* 12:36). Here the focus is on their impact in the world. (Cf. Eph. 5:9–10).

I John states that believers are "called *(klēthōmen)* children of God."

> See what love the Father has given us, that we should be called children of God; and so we are. (I John 3:1)

The expression is introduced in such a way as to suggest that for the author and his readers this is the normative designation for the believers. That believers were not always called "Christians" is clear from Acts 11:26. An early designation for them was those "belonging to the Way" (Acts 9:2). The expression "the children of God" may well antedate the designation "Christian," for it has historic Old Testament roots. The church often took over and used for itself expressions that formerly were applied exclusively to Israel. We see a clear example of this in I Peter 2:9–10, where several such expressions are appropriated. In the Old Testament the word used is normally "sons" rather than "children." John prefers to keep the word "son" exclusively for Jesus (except in John 12:36, cited above). Examples of Old Testament usage are Isa. 1:2, where Israel is spoken of as God's "sons," Jer. 10:20 (LXX), "My sons and my sheep are not . . . ," Hos. 1:10 (Hebrew Text, 2:1), "They shall be called Sons of the Living God," and Deut. 14:1, "You are the sons of the Lord your God."

John's use of the word "sons" instead of "children" on one occasion (12:36) may reflect traditional usage, for the phrase "sons of light" is prominent in the Dead Sea Scrolls. John's Gospel centers on Jesus as the Christ, the Son of God (20:30–31), and John's theology consistently uses "son" *(huios)* for Jesus and "children" *(tekna)* for believers. I John also has a penchant for the diminutive word *teknia* ("little children," I John 2:1,12,28; 3:7,18; 4:4; 5:21; cf. John 13:33). Except for the above references the word *teknia* occurs in only one place in the New Testament, namely, Gal. 4:19. The leaning toward the diminutive word may emerge from the special pastoral role in which the author of I John stood in relation to the people to whom he was writing. It suggests that the writer is a mature Christian leader, possibly of advanced years.

The people (ho laos). In one of the passages that was

considered in the study of the expression "the children of God" in the Gospel of John there also occurs the phrase, "It is expedient for you that one man should die for the people" (11:50). The context makes it clear that the author has in mind here not the Jewish nation but "the people of God." The Jewish nation he refers to as "the nation" *(to ethnos)* or "the whole nation" *(holon to ethnos)*. The phrase "the people" in v. 50 is parallel to "the children of God" in v. 52. The death of Jesus is for "the people." The high priest, in keeping with a consistent pattern in John, speaks more than he knows. He has unwittingly predicted the atoning significance of the death of Jesus. He does this because "he did not say this of his own accord" (v. 51). Rather, he was used by God to prophesy. Hence, Jesus' death for "the people" is his atoning death. In the New Testament the word *laos* ("people") is appropriated for the church (e.g., Rom. 9:25–26; I Peter 2:9; etc.). Caiaphas' prophecy is repeated in John 18:14, again using the word *laos*. It seems clear, therefore, that in John the phrase "the people" as used in 11:50 and 18:14 is a technical term and refers to the church. It is the new people of God composed of both Jews and Gentiles.[2]

His own. The expression "his own" has two very different meanings in John. In 1:11 the reference is to the Jewish nation. It reads:

> He came to his own home *(ta idia,* literally, "his own things"),
> and his own people *(hoi idioi)* received him not.

Here the author is reminding his readers that though Jesus emerged out of Israel, Israel as a people did not respond to him. The writer reflects his knowledge of the sharp division that existed at the time of his writing between Israel and the church.

In 13:1, however, the reference to "his own" is clearly to Jesus' disciples:

Now before the feast of the Passover, when Jesus knew that his hour had come to depart out of this world to the Father, having loved his own *(hoi idioi)* who were in the world, he loved them to the end.

The expression *hoi idioi* implies membership, ownership, or belonging. Sheep, for example, that belong to a given shepherd are referred to as "his own" (10:4). It is used to refer to fellow Christians:

When they were released they went to their friends *(hoi idioi)* . . . (Acts 4:23)

. . . and that none of his friends *(hoi idioi)* should be prevented from attending to his needs. (Acts 24:23)

It is also used of one's relatives:

If any one does not provide for his relatives *(hoi idioi)*, and especially for his own family, he has disowned the faith and is worse than an unbeliever. (I Tim. 5:8)

Bultmann points out that the expression became a "specifically Gnostic designation."[3] As John uses the term, it refers to the disciples. Since in the parable of the sheep "his own" (10:3–4) appears to include other sheep who would be brought into the flock (10:16), it seems proper to conclude that for John "his own" can properly be extended to refer, by implication, to all believers. This would include, therefore, the writer and the believers to whom he now writes. They too belong to Jesus and are a part of "his own." Once again we have an expression that is equivalent to Christian or believer. It is a designation, in other words, for the church.

One flock, one shepherd. One of the most important images used by John for the church and its relationship to Jesus is that of the sheep and the shepherd (10:1–18). This image of the people of God as a flock under a divine shepherd is deeply rooted in the religious heritage of Israel. Yahweh was Israel's shepherd (Ps. 23:1) and Israel was God's flock (Ezek., ch. 34). Jeremiah foresaw the day when the flock of Israel, then sorely neglected, would be properly protected and provided for by a shepherd who would not, as some were then doing, destroy and scatter the flock (Jer. 23:1-4). Other Old Testament passages that use the same imagery include Ps. 74:1; 78:52,70-72; 100:3; Isa. 40:11; Jer. 31:10.

Christ is the good shepherd who lays down his life for the sheep (10:11,15). The sheep follow him, for they know his voice (10:4). The parable affirms that this "fold" is an ever-widening fellowship which embraces "other sheep," presumably Gentiles being so designated (10:16). The flock-shepherd motif shows strong Hebraic ties. Bultmann,[4] however, has noted similarities to the image of the shepherd in Mandaean literature and argues that John's parable has been influenced by the Gnostic tradition. C. H. Dodd[5] believes the influence has gone in the opposite direction. Dodd's view has greater acceptance today than Bultmann's.

Nils Dahl[6] sees in this parable a close analogy between the followers of Jesus and the people of Israel. There is, as he puts it, "a continuity between Israel and the church." Cullmann also recognizes the emphasis in John upon continuity between Israel and the church. Jesus came "to his own," that is, to Israel. "Salvation is from the Jews" (4:22). The incarnate Jesus, argues Cullmann,[7] is the center of the realization of the divine plan of salvation. This ties the Old and the New Testament together. Both Dahl and Cullmann challenge Bultmann for not recognizing sufficiently John's teaching here with regard to "salvation history." They maintain that Bultmann's stress on an existential interpretation of the gospel has led him to minimize its tie to the Old Testament.

The vine and the branches. Another crucial symbol for the church in John is that of the vine and the branches (ch. 15).

This imagery is also a time-honored one in Israel's history. Israel was viewed as God's planting (Ps. 80:8–16; Isa. 5:1–7; 27:2–6; Jer. 2:21; Ezek. 19:10–14). We read, for example,

> For the vineyard of the LORD of hosts
> is the house of Israel,
> and the men of Judah
> his pleasant planting.
>
> (Isa. 5:7)

The relationship suggested by John implies that the believer must be joined to Christ if he is to remain spiritually alive. John writes:

> Abide in me, and I in you. As the branch cannot bear fruit by itself, unless it abides in the vine, neither can you, unless you abide in me. I am the vine, you are the branches. He who abides in me, and I in him, he it is that bears much fruit, for apart from me you can do nothing. If a man does not abide in me, he is cast forth as a branch and withers; and the branches are gathered, thrown into the fire and burned. (15:4–6)

In other words, John is talking of a *vital* relationship in the literal root meaning of that word. It is a matter of *life* and death. Jesus is the source and channel of life for the branches, that is, the believers. When the branches "remain" in the vine, life-giving energy flows through the vine to the branches. This guarantees both health and fruit-bearing. When the branches are separated from the vine, an inevitable result follows: the branches simply wither and dry up. Since no nourishment reaches them, they will bear no fruit.

The church finds its origin, meaning, strength, and ultimate purpose in the person of Jesus Christ. Apart from him, John is saying, the church has neither life nor message, neither purpose nor mission, and is powerless for service. In vital union with him, however, there will be life and fruitfulness. This is the pastoral concern which prompts the author of the Gospel of John to instruct and exhort his readers.

Expressions Concerning the Church

"Even so I send you." The Gospel of John implies the existence of a community of believers by its stress on mission and outreach. Jesus is quoted:

> Peace be with you. As the Father has sent me, *even so I send you.* (20:21)

This appears to be John's equivalent to the Great Commission (Matt. 28:19–20). This emphasis on missionary expansion permeates the gospel. It is implied in Jesus' prayer,

> I do not pray for these only, but also for those who believe in me through their word. (17:20)

Jesus died "to gather into one the children of God who are scattered abroad" (11:52).

In John, Jesus does not come only to the house of Israel. He has been sent by the Father because the Father loves "the world" (3:16). *Anyone* who receives him can become one of "the children of God" (1:12). Even the Samaritan fields are white and ready for harvest (4:35). It is from the lips of non-Jews, from Samaritans, that the great confession is made. "This is indeed the Savior of the world" (4:42). In being "lifted up," Jesus drew "all men" to himself (12:32). The Book of Signs reaches its close only when "the Greeks" have come to the point of wanting to come and see Jesus (12:20–21).

The fishing scene in John 21:1–11 appears also to symbolize the missionary outreach of the disciples. Luke 5:1–11, which is in many ways parallel to the account in John 21:1–11, ties the fishing of the disciples with missionary outreach. It concludes with the statement, "Do not be afraid; henceforth you will be catching men" (Luke 5:10). In John 21:3 it states that they toiled all night but "caught nothing." This is reminiscent of the words of John 15:5, "Apart from

me you can do nothing." Jesus then instructs them where to
fish and the catch is so great they can get the net to shore only
with great difficulty. The implied lesson is that the church, if
it is to be effective in mission, can do so only in and through
Jesus. Without him all efforts will be in vain.

Mission implies a community to which new believers
become attached. Here they are instructed and built up in
their faith. John's Gospel is part of this instruction. In all of
this a gathered church provides the background for John's
exhortation to his readers to embrace the universal mission of
God in Jesus.

"I chose you." Jesus' disciples were "chosen" by him. He
states,

> You did not choose me, but I chose you and appointed you
> that you should go and bear fruit and that your fruit should
> abide. (John 15:16)

The verb that John uses is *eklegomai,* "choose," "select." It is
related to the expression found in I Peter 2:9, "a chosen race"
(genos eklekton). The issue of election is involved here and it
reflects John's understanding of the church. The disciples
were chosen, selected by Jesus. Rather, they were given to
him by the Father (John 17:6, 12). Clearly, however, the
disciples are, for John, representatives of the church. As one
writer correctly puts it, they

> represent the Church or are the Church in miniature so that
> what he says about the disciples he understands about the
> Church.[8]

As the author quotes Jesus' teachings to his disciples he is
simultaneously (and primarily) giving instruction to the
readers who constitute the church in Asia Minor in the
vicinity of Ephesus. History and application join hands
under the skillful and pastoral guidance of John's creative

sculpturing. In the disciples he sees the church. In the words addressed to the disciples we hear more than the words of Jesus; we also hear "what the Spirit says to the churches" (Rev. 3:22).

"He will guide you." John stresses that Jesus remains with his church through the Holy Spirit. Christ, who is the source of the Spirit (7:39), sends the Spirit as the strengthener and guide of the believers (14:16–18,26; 15:26,27; 16:7–15). The gift of the Spirit came to the believers after the resurrection (20:22). The Spirit does not speak about himself but continues the work of Jesus. John has a dynamic concept of the ongoing work of Jesus in the church through his Spirit. He quotes Jesus:

> I have yet many things to say to you, but you cannot bear them now. When the Spirit of truth comes, he will guide you into all the truth; for he will not speak on his own authority, but whatever he hears he will speak, and he will declare to you the things that are to come. (16:12–13)

Jesus said, "I will not leave you desolate; I will come to you" (14:18). Here we see John's conviction that the church has not been left an orphan. It has in its midst the presence of Jesus through the Holy Spirit to guide it in the challenges and demands of the present and the future. Whereas some writers in the New Testament, such as Luke, find their answer in tradition, John finds his security in the Spirit of Truth. Luke speaks of that which was "delivered to us by those who from the beginning were eyewitnesses and ministers of the word" (Luke 1:2). John looks to the Spirit, who "will guide you into all the truth" (16:13). There is a different tone here. Rather than stressing tradition, John stresses a living principle. Jesus, through the Spirit, "is the vital principle of the whole Christian community." [9] John provides a balance to any who might put undue stress on tradition. The Johannine and

Lucan emphases reflect diversity in the New Testament perspective and perhaps they provide a proper balance between two extremes. As Raymond E. Brown has put it:

> A community that depends totally on the Spirit as an operative factor I suspect will wander away from a long and God-given sense of tradition. A community that depends totally on tradition, that tests everything only on whether it is faithful to what was handed down to us, will become a community that maybe cannot speak to its time and make the kind of changes necessary for its time. . . . Without the two in tension you are not going to get a Christian picture.[10]

"That they may all be one." The unity of the believers is a major theme in the prayer of Jesus in ch. 17. It is especially stressed in vs. 11, 21, and 23. This section of John is part of the farewell discourses and has the character of teaching more than it does of prayer, although it is cast in the mold of the latter. It really combines an exhortation for unity with a summary of the theological message of the Gospel of John. One might call it a didactic prayer. Raymond E. Brown[11] identifies the literary genre we have here as a farewell discourse such as is found in Genesis for Jacob (Gen., ch. 49) and in the pseudepigraphical book, the Testament of the Twelve Patriarchs.

Since the unity that is prayed for is compared to the unity that exists between the Father and the Son (17:11,21), a unity of mind and purpose would seem to be part of the unity that is sought. In the prayer Jesus stresses that he has always done the Father's will (17:4). But more than a spiritual unity of this kind seems to be involved. As Brown puts it:

> The fact that the unity has to be visible enough to challenge the world to believe in Jesus (17:21,23) seems to militate against a purely spiritual union. If we interpret 17:21-23 in the light of 10:16 with its stress on one sheep herd, one shepherd, then it becomes plausible that unity involves

community, even though the latter idea is not explicit in 17. Certainly in the *mashal* of the vine and the branches, which has the same Last Discourse context as the prayer of 17, the notion of unity with Jesus involves community (15:5,6).[12]

That the Johannine community has some sense of self-identity is apparent from a look at I John where some have left the group and now no longer gather with them in worship. We read,

They went out from us, but they were not of us; for if they had been of us, they would have continued with us; but they went out, that it might be plain that they all are not of us. (I John 2:19)

Is John's Understanding of the Church "Institutional"?

The question that has arisen at this point is to what extent the Johannine church partakes of the nature of an institution. Furthermore, the issue has been raised as to whether or not this community stands in the so-called "mainstream" (if there was something in the first century that could be so identified) of the church? We shall examine this matter briefly.

John's silence about many aspects of church life and organization has led some New Testament interpreters to view John as standing in opposition to the institutional church.[13] The stress is on the individual "standing, under the working of the Spirit, face to face with God. No one can teach him, and no one can correct him. . . . There are no longer any special ministries." [14] The same writer concludes that in John there is no church order at all.[15] The church is the church "only in so far as it lives 'in' the Son and he in it." [16]

This view of John has also been expressed by Bultmann, who wrote: "No specifically ecclesiological interest can be

detected. There is no interest in cult or organization." [17]
Bultmann admits that there is a lively interest in the church in
this Gospel but says that "the Johannine terminology pertain-
ing to the Church comes . . . from the area of Gnostic
thought." [18] Is this valid?

Nils Dahl disagrees. He argues that John is more closely
tied to the Old Testament and to the Christian church of his
day than either Bultmann or Schweizer have recognized.[19]
He raises such questions as the following: Is it true that there
is no organization? Is not the author himself a presbyter (II
John 1; III John 1)? Was not Peter recommissioned for a
pastoral role (John 21:15–19)? Is not some kind of authority
implied in the following charge?

> If you forgive the sins of any, they are forgiven; if you retain
> the sins of any, they are retained. (20:23)

Dahl goes on to argue that in attacking the abuse of authority
seen in the person of Diotrephes (III John 9), the author does
not thereby attack all church order or organization. The
writer himself complains that Diotrephes "does not acknowledge my authority." The implication is that Diotrephes
should acknowledge it, and his failure to do so stems from the
very independence of spirit of which Bultmann accuses the
writer to be guilty.

R. Schnackenburg also regards as a distortion of the facts
the view that John's Gospel is an example of "an individual,
spiritualized, even 'mystical' Christianity." [20] While it is true
that the chief interest of John is Christology, the "Church in
fact is assigned a quite definite position in the work of
salvation." [21] "Spirit and life," maintains Schnackenburg,
"are only conveyed and preserved, are only operative and
fruitful in the community." [22] Elsewhere Schnackenburg
writes:

> It is in the Church that the Holy Spirit teaches through the
> apostolic word and brings to mind all that Jesus said (cf.

14:26; 16:13 f.), and it is through the Church that he "convinces" the unbelieving world (16:8–11; cf. 15:26 f.). . . .

There is no indication that the evangelist isolates himself and the group to which he belongs from the apostolic missions of the universal Church.[23]

Bultmann and Schnackenburg appear to represent opposite poles in this discussion. Has Bultmann sought to remove John too far from the rest of the Christians of the first century? Has Schnackenburg, on the other hand, failed to give adequate recognition to the diversity in New Testament theology which the Gospel of John presents? There certainly does seem to be a very different emphasis in John. Structure is not primary in his thinking. He stands far removed from such emphases on structure as found, for example, in the pastoral letters. He focuses instead on "believing," on "abiding in" Jesus, and on the personal dynamic presence and guidance of the Holy Spirit. To say that all of this is communicated through the institutional church is to incorporate into John ideas that have been derived elsewhere. If this was John's thought, we have to infer it since he does not himself stress it.

C. F. D. Moule has given what seems to be a more balanced judgment. He acknowledges the personal thrust of John's emphasis over against an institutional perspective. He writes:

This is the Gospel, par excellence, of the approach of the single soul to God: this is the part of Scripture to which one turns first when trying to direct an enquirer to his own, personal appropriation of salvation. Here, then, is an emphasis which is precious in the extreme. Only, it is not a total, inclusive view. It is as one-sided (in depth) as Luke-Acts tend to be (in breadth). The thinker who most organically and most profoundly combines the two planes is Paul.[24]

Individualism, versus institutionalism, is primary in John.

Is the Gospel at the same time anti-ecclesiastical? This is Ernst Käsemann's contention. He regards John as a "remarkable counteroffensive" against a movement in the church toward a highly structured institution.[25] The latter form of church government he finds exemplified in the pastoral letters. In I Tim. 3:1–13, for instance, detailed instructions are given regarding the proper qualifications for overseers and deacons. The Gospel of John neither describes nor mentions such church offices. Käsemann goes on to say:

The tradition of the apostles is nowhere directly and unmistakably encountered as such.[26]

Käsemann interprets this silence as Johannine opposition to the established church. He writes:

The fact that only occasional glances are cast in the direction of the Church's situation and that many points at issue run counter to it should be interpreted as polemic on the part of John.[27]

Raymond E. Brown notes the distinctiveness of John's views but believes that Käsemann's thesis proves too much. It is based unduly on arguments from silence. John's views are compared by Käsemann primarily with the letters of Paul rather than with the Synoptic Gospels. After all, John chose to use the Gospel model as the one he would follow in his writing. The diversity of genre and purpose (between a gospel and a letter) accounts, says Brown, for several omissions in John. Brown writes:

From the symbolism of the vine and the branches, for instance,

one may conclude that the evangelist wishes to stress union with Jesus, and this emphasis fits the purpose of the Gospel. But to go beyond that and posit that the evangelist is opposed to or indifferent to a structured Church is risky indeed.[28]

Brown, like Moule, notes the stress on individualism in John. He states:

A structured Johannine "church" there may be, but that church must be subordinate to Jesus. The Church in itself is not the source of salvation; only the Spirit of Jesus gives life.[29]

For John it is the inner life of believers and their relationship to one another which is his primary concern rather than ecclesiastical structure. In discussing how the believers are to live, he emphasizes believing, the gift of the Spirit, love, abiding in Christ, being witnesses, and feeding the sheep. Instead of stressing structure and authority, John demonstrates by the foot-washing scene the proper attitude and behavior that should characterize the relationships between believers.

Käsemann has properly pointed out diversity in John's emphasis. John's concerns are by no means the same as those of the writer of the pastoral letters. To find a deliberate polemic, however, expresses the difference very strongly and it seems too strongly. John's intent may have been of the nature of a corrective. This would not imply a desire to set aside such structure as was then in existence.

Baptism and the Lord's Supper. Bultmann finds in the Gospel of John three passages that refer to baptism or to the Lord's Supper. These are 3:5; 6:51b–58; 19:34–35. These, he argues, are later additions to the text, having been added by an ecclesiastical redactor. This person added them, in Bultmann's judgment, in order to make John conform more closely to the teachings of the Synoptic Gospels (and of the wider church) on the subject of the sacraments. It is Bultmann's contention that the original author was basically nonsacramental. Bultmann writes:

> One can therefore explain the facts only by concluding that, while the Evangelist came to terms with ecclesiastical practice in regard to baptism and the Lord's Supper, it remained suspect to him, because of its misuse, and that is why he has

made no mention of it. The truth is that the sacraments are superfluous for him.[30]

There is no textual problem with these passages. Bultmann's objections stem from his theological understanding of John rather than from manuscript variants. A number of interpreters, including Eduard Schweizer, remain unconvinced by Bultmann's contention that these verses are later additions.[31] The Gospel indicates that John the Baptist practiced water baptism (1.24–28, 3:23; 4:1–2; 10:40). He himself distinguished between what he was doing and what the Messiah would do when he came. He would baptize people "with the Holy Spirit" (1:33). That Jesus supported baptism is stated in 3:22 and 4:1. The writer then adds the comment, "although Jesus himself did not baptize, but only his disciples" (4:2). The author of the Fourth Gospel is therefore aware that baptism was practiced from the beginning of Jesus' ministry, that Jesus' disciples engaged in the practice, and that they apparently did so with Jesus' approval. For the writer, however, this is only a first step. More significant than water baptism is the baptism that Jesus gives. This is the baptism with the Spirit.

Beyond these few passages the theme of baptism may also be implied in 3:5 and 19:34–35. In the former it is stated that one must be "born of water and the Spirit." "Born of water," if it applies to baptism, would imply cleansing, as baptism normally does in the New Testament. It was the rite that marked the initiation of the believer into the fellowship of the Christians in the first century. John would remind his readers, however, that there is also the need to be "born of the Spirit." In other words, the external rite in and of itself is not enough. This would suggest that he would repudiate any idea that the practice of the sacrament of baptism in and of itself was what was called for. John stressed personal believing and personal receiving of the Spirit. His concept

was dynamic and vital. Perhaps in stressing this in the way
he does he is seeking to correct an improper interpretation
which has tended to mechanize and institutionalize discipleship.

Another important passage is 19:34–35. Following the
spear thrust into the side of Jesus, the writer tells us with great
earnestness and with apparent theological overtones, "And at
once there came out blood and water." That this has some
special meaning in the thought of the writer appears to be
supported by a somewhat similar statement in the First
Letter. There we read:

> This is he who came by water and blood, Jesus Christ, not
> with the water only but with the water and the blood. . . .
> There are three witnesses, the Spirit, the water, and the blood;
> and these three agree. (I John 5:6,8)

Clearly in I John the reference seems to be to baptism and
communion. What else can it possibly mean? In the light of
this the statement in 19:34–35 may very well be intended to
have symbolic significance.

Some see in these verses an anti-Gnostic thrust. It stresses,
in this view, the real humanity of Jesus. One wonders,
however, why Jesus' humanity could not have been more
clearly and more frequently stressed throughout the Gospel if
this was one of the author's concerns. Anti-Gnosticism seems
clear in I John. It is not so clear in the Gospel.

Water and blood would symbolize cleansing and the
atonement. We must be washed by Jesus if we are to have
any part in him, according to John (13:9–10; cf. 9:7).

It is a peculiarity of the Fourth Gospel that the establishment of the Lord's Supper is not recorded in this Gospel.
This is all the more strange in view of the fact that no Gospel
gives more attention and space to the account of the Lord in
the upper room with his disciples than does the Gospel of
John. Where a person would expect to find the account of

the institution of the Lord's Supper, there is instead the presentation of the foot washing. For some reason the author deliberately omits any reference at this point to the Eucharist. He does indicate that the conversations do take place during and following a supper (13:2). That the author knew about the Eucharist becomes abundantly clear from the manner in which it is referred to indirectly in ch. 6. Here the author uses terminology that is clearly related to and derived from the observance of the Lord's Supper. This is evident from such eucharistic terms as "to give thanks" (6:11,23); "to give bread," "to eat," "on behalf of" (6:51), and "to drink" and "blood" (6:53–54). There is no suggestion that John wishes to dispense with the observance of the Lord's Supper. John's discussion appears to reflect rather a concern about how the sacrament should be interpreted in the Christian community.

There is a certain polemical and hostile tone to this dialogue in ch. 6. The tension does not seem to relate to the time of Jesus. As G. H. C. Macgregor aptly observed:

> The Eucharistic discussion (6:32–59), which would be quite impossible in Jesus' own day before the sacrament was even instituted, becomes intelligible when related to a later Jewish attack upon Christian sacramental teaching.[32]

Macgregor expands this statement by saying that polemical dialogues such as this one,

> suggest the disputes between Jew and Christian of a later age, when Christian theology had been definitely formulated and Christianity and Judaism faced each other as rivals.[33]

This section of John (and much of the rest of the book) appears to reflect church-synagogue tensions. They emerge, in other words, from the discussions that were going on among Jews and Christians in a city in the Diaspora. The Jews were arguing against the claims of the Christians that

Jesus was the Messiah and that through believing in him a person received life. They seem also to have rejected and presumably ridiculed the claims of the Christians regarding the Lord's Supper where believers gathered to partake of the elements that represented "the body and blood of Christ." Such an idea was repugnant and offensive to the Jews. The acrimony of the dialogue that went on seems to be reflected in the bald statement:

> Truly, truly, I say to you, unless you eat the flesh of the Son of man and drink his blood, you have no life in you; he who eats my flesh and drinks my blood has eternal life, and I will raise him up at the last day. For my flesh is food indeed, and my blood is drink indeed. (6:53–55)

The conflict that characterizes this discussion in ch. 6 is continued and intensified in chs. 7 through 9. In these chapters the various objections to the claims of the Christians concerning Jesus are presented and answers given. These are chapters defending the Christian Christology as it had developed.[34]

John does not reject either baptism or the Lord's Supper. He acknowledges them and defends them against Jewish objections. At the time, the lack of prominence given to them indicates that for him they are not of primary importance in and by themselves. We must understand the verse

> Unless you eat the flesh of the Son of man and drink his blood, you have no life in you (6:53)

in the light of the two other verses in the context, namely:

> He who believes has eternal life (6:47)

and:

> It is the spirit that gives life, the flesh is of no avail; the words that I have spoken to you are spirit and life. (6:63)

Colwell and Titus conclude that while the practice of

baptism and the observance of the Lord's Supper are not repudiated by John, the author does reject a strictly sacramental interpretation of them. They write:

> John repudiates sacramentalism, Pauline or otherwise! Apparently, it is not congenial to his religious outlook. Why? Because it violated his dynamic concept of religion. For him the Spirit is functionally and dynamically present in the church's experience leading its members into ever-enlarging experiences of awareness of meaning and value. The sacramental view of religion is consequently too mechanical for him to embrace it. We would go so far as to say that the Fourth Gospel represents a reaction to an increasing suppression of spontaneous religious experience through the substitution of an *ex opere operato* sacramental ritual.[35]

Oscar Cullmann similarly argues that John wishes to affirm that without faith, which is a gift of God, the eating of the bread and the drinking of the wine have no effect.[36]

There is the possibility that 6:51–58 is a Johannine interpolation.[37] If so, these verses are a second bread of life discourse parallel to the first one (6:35–50). The passage 6:51–58 is clearly congenial to a highly sacramental interpretation. It must, however, be viewed in the light of the verses cited earlier, namely, 6:47 and 63. If added later, it represents a sacramental interpolation which is not expressed earlier in the discourse. If original, it reflects current debate but is presented in the context of a Johannine theology which tempers the strictly mechanistic view which a literal exegesis might give to the passage. The dynamic, personal quality of believing, plus the movement of the Spirit which is free like the blowing of the wind (3:8), repudiates such a view of the sacraments. This kind of interpretation would be alien to the creative dynamism of John's understanding of the new life of Jesus.

Believers and the world. In the Gospel of John the

followers of Jesus are viewed as a group that has been chosen "out of the world" (15:19). Therefore the world hates them. They face hatred (17:14), persecution (15:20; 16:33), and (if Jews) excommunication from the synagogue (9:22; 12:42; 16:2). Such statements in John reflect the tensions present several decades after the time of Jesus. The Christian community is "locked in combat with the synagogue." [38] A formal excommunication appears to be referred to. This seems to have been formulated by Judaism through the Jamnia academy about A.D. 85.[39] It is another indication of the sharp distinction that now exists between Christians and Jews and between a Christian congregation and a Jewish one. Each claims to be "the people of God." Each group arrogates prerogatives to itself and denies them to the other. In the process the Christian community gained a growing self-conscious awareness of its identity. It had become the church, something quite distinct from Judaism and the synagogue. John wrote in order to strengthen the church in the face of its challenges and opportunities.

6

~~~~~~~~~~~~~~~~~~~~~~~~~~~~~~~~~~~~~~

Believe

Among the most familiar and characteristic words in Johannine vocabulary are the expressions "to believe" and "to know." While in normal English usage the meanings of these words would be quite distinct, in The Gospel According to John they are closely interrelated. Very often they are treated as synonyms. At other times the meanings are different.

In the Fourth Gospel faith and knowledge partake of a vibrant quality which involves the whole man and which is centered in a religious experience that can never be reduced to a formal acceptance of creedal beliefs or to the acquisition of factual information concerning God. In this chapter we shall examine John's understanding of "believing."

John's view of faith is dynamic. He writes his Gospel in order that men may believe and that believing they may have life. Throughout he uses the verbal form of the word with great frequency but totally avoids the noun "faith" (or "belief"). Seldom does he use the verb absolutely, that is, without an object. If an object is not explicitly stated, the context makes it clear that it is implied. The act of "believing" is consistently directed toward either God or Jesus. Sometimes it is Jesus as a person that is the object of faith, and occasionally it is his works or words. Jesus is the manifestation of the Father, and all believing is intimately tied to the acceptance of this affirmation. This is the response that the author seeks to evoke in his readers.

The centrality of faith for this Gospel can be seen by comparing the frequency of the use of the words "to believe" and "belief" ("faith") in the four Gospels:

	Matt.	Mark	Luke	John	I John
pisteuein ("to believe")	11	14	9	98	9
pistis ("belief," "faith")	8	5	11	0	1

Of the ninety-eight occurrences of "to believe" in John, seventy-four are in the first twelve chapters of the book. This is the section that contains the Book of Signs where the miracles are presented to demonstrate that Jesus is the Christ. The appeal for believing is strongest here. Once the author comes to 13:1, Jesus is with "his own" and these have already believed. Hence there is a shift to new concerns. The discipleship which begins with believing must move on to growth in other areas such as love, obedience, and service.

In his statement of purpose, as given in John 20:30–31, the author has given "believing" a central place. For John, believing is Christ-centered. What is involved in this act of believing? Peter's reply to a question asked by Jesus helps to focus on what is uppermost in the author's thought. Peter replies to Jesus' question, "Will you also go away?" with the words:

Lord, to whom shall we go? You have the words of eternal

life; and we have believed, and have come to know, that you
are the Holy One of God. (6:68–69)

Believing in Jesus involves an acknowledgment that Jesus has
been sent into the world by God to reveal the Father.
Believing in Jesus means to recognize and to accept the fact
that he is the one who manifests the Father, that he has come
to do the Father's will, and that through him men may come
to know God.

One of the distinctive ways in which the verb "to believe"
(pisteuein) is used in The Gospel According to John is with
the added preposition *eis*, which means "in" or "into." The
addition of this preposition normally suggests motion toward
something. In its use here it connotes a commitment *to* Jesus
as the Christ. It implies a dynamic personal commitment that
moves the idea beyond mere intellectual assent. Raymond E.
Brown expresses the connotation well with these words:

> Thus, *pisteuein eis* may be defined in terms of an active
> commitment to a person and, in particular, to Jesus. It
> involves much more than trust in Jesus or confidence in him;
> it is an acceptance of Jesus and of what he claims to be and a
> dedication of one's life to him. The commitment is not
> emotional but involves a willingness to respond to God's
> demands as they are presented in and by Jesus.[1]

The expression *pisteuein eis* is found thirty-six times in
John, three times in I John, and only eight times in the rest of
the New Testament. There is no parallel for this usage in the
Septuagint (the Greek translation of the Old Testament) or in
secular Greek. It emerged to express what was at the heart of
John's message. In normal Greek usage the verb *pisteuein*
meant simply credence or intellectual assent and acceptance.
In order to make clear that John meant more than this and
intended also the thought of personal trust or reliance, a new
manner of expression came into prominence.[2]

John uses a number of other verbs to express much the

same idea as "believing." These he treats as basically synonyms. They include such words as: to come, to follow, to enter, to drink, to accept, to receive, to love, to hear.

Bultmann points out that for John believing proceeds from "hearing" (5:24), or even directly *is* hearing, provided this is not just physical hearing but a positive response to God's call through Jesus.[3] John quotes Jesus as follows:

> Every one who has heard and learned from the Father comes to me. (6:45)

H. Schlier[4] also interprets John's understanding of faith as primarily a "hearing." He illustrates this by referring to the Johannine image of the sheep hearing the voice of the shepherd (10:3,8,16,27). It is a "critical" hearing which distinguishes the voice of Jesus from all the other voices which press in to be heard. Through such "hearing," persons now receive life:

> Truly, truly, I say to you, the hour is coming, and now is, when the dead will hear the voice of the Son of God, and those who hear will live. (5:25)

Schlier writes:

> Hearing not only inaugurates faith, but faith finds its fulfillment in hearing. Finally a person may also say that faith is secured in hearing. This is the case when hearing is the hearing of obedience (in keeping with 12:46 ff.).[5]

Another prominent synonym for "believing" in John is "seeing." G. L. Phillips placed the four Greek words used for "seeing" in the Fourth Gospel *(blepein, theōrein, theasthai, and horan)* in an ascending scale, which he then completed with a fifth word, namely, "believing" *(pisteuein).* He argued that each word suggested a stronger vision or knowledge and that the author of the Fourth Gospel intended that each word be stronger than the one before it in the list. "Believing" is viewed as "the climax of this series."[6] This interpretation seems somewhat forced. John frequently uses words that are synonyms, with no apparent difference intended. It is part of his style of writing. Bultmann views the various verbs for "seeing" as found in John to be "without distinction." [7] Bultmann's comment at this point is helpful. He writes:

> The parallelism—or rather, identity—of believing, hearing, and seeing indicates by itself that sight to John is not mystical contemplation. Sight, or seeing, is to him faith's perception: faith recognizes in the historical Jesus the "truth" and "life" which only he transmits and which therefore are not perceptible to direct contemplation. [8]

A. Schlatter[9] interprets the use of the words "hearing" and "seeing" in John to be related to the two gifts of Jesus, namely, his word and his work. Believers "hear" his word and they "see" his work. In the first case it is a hearing of response and obedience. In the second instance the seeing is a recognition and acknowledgment that these are the works of God and that Jesus, by what he does, reveals the Father.

H. Wenz[10] has written an article on the words spoken to Thomas after Thomas' confession of faith:

> Have you believed because you have seen me? Blessed are those who have not seen and yet believe. (20:29)

Jesus' statement about "believing" without "seeing" does not mean that the resurrection appearances of Jesus are of relative value, says Wenz. John handles his tradition so freely that he could have left the appearances out if he had wanted to. Seeing is important for John. The once-for-all believing through seeing is appropriate for the first chosen witnesses; believing without seeing befits those who are born later.

Paul's and James's antithesis between works and faith is not a part of John's debate. For John, the work of God is to believe in Jesus (6:29). The opponents of John are not the Judaizers of Galatia but "the Jews." "The Jews" represent the hierarchy at Jerusalem and presumedly the synagogue leadership at the time of writing. John seeks to show how Jesus replaces the old order with the new. While the law was given by Moses, grace and truth have come through Jesus Christ (1:17). Again we read,

> Truly, truly, I say to you, it was not Moses who gave you the bread from heaven; my Father gives you the true bread from heaven. (6:32)

The rival faith of Judaism and to a lesser extent the rival faith of the Samaritans is presented as having been supplanted by Jesus. The day has arrived when men are to worship God neither at Jerusalem nor at Mt. Gerizim; they are to worship in spirit and in truth (4:21–24). It is another way of saying what Jesus says later in the words:

> I am the way, and the truth, and the life; no one comes to the Father, but by me. (14:6)

The total avoidance of the noun "faith" in The Gospel According to John seems to be deliberate. It may be that the noun form suggested too static an understanding of what John meant by "believing." He wished to highlight the dynamic quality of personal commitment and John's verbal use was more effective for this than the noun would have been. Another possible explanation is that John was displeased with the use of the nouns "faith" *(pistis)* and "knowledge" *(gnōsis)* in a developing movement which came to be known as Gnosticism. Since he avoids the word "knowledge" as well as "faith," this explanation may have merit. It is interesting that the noun "faith" occurs once in I John where we read:

> For whatever is born of God overcomes the world; and this is the victory that overcomes the world, our faith. (I John 5:4)

Does this divergence from the regular Johannine pattern

support the view of those who maintain that I John is from a different author than the Gospel of John even though they share very much in common in terms of both vocabulary and ideas?

Bultmann[11] has made the very helpful suggestion that *pisteuein* takes over, in Johannine language, an element of the meaning of the Hebrew word for knowing *(yd')* which the Greek word for knowing *(ginōskein)* did not possess. In Hebrew, *yd'* carried the connotation of acknowledging God by way of submission to his will. Some of this idea is included in John's use of "believing" *(pisteuein)*.

The interrelationship of "seeing," "believing," and "knowing" in John is very close. Consequently Bultmann can write:

Sight, then, is *the knowing* that is peculiar to faith. Hence "see" and "know" can be combined or be used as alternatives (14:7,9,17; I John 3:6). . . . *Faith is genuine* only insofar as it is *knowing* faith.[12]

"Knowing God" is eternal life (17:3). The same verse also says that eternal life is "knowing Jesus Christ," whom God has sent. The two are inseparably linked for John. Once again we see Jesus as the one who reveals the Father. He who has the Son has the Father, and vice versa. "Believing" in Jesus is the total response of the whole person to God as he has made himself known in the Son. It is openness to the Spirit who blows where he wills even as the wind sweeps across the hills of Galilee. It includes a willingness to confess the doctrine that Jesus is the Son of God, but it is more than that. It implies obedience to Jesus' commands. It is demonstrated by love for the brethren. It demands concern for the unity of the community of faith. It involves a willingness to assume the role of the servant as Jesus himself did, not only in the upper room but at the cross. It calls for feeding the sheep and for "abiding" day by day in "the vine" so that the spiritual life which has been begun may be nurtured and developed and that the believer may "bear fruit."

Clearly this is a very dynamic concept of the Christian life. Dogma is not enough. The author is not satisfied with a simple verbal affirmation of belief. He calls for discipleship. That means to "hear" the voice of the shepherd and "to follow" the shepherd wherever he leads. A person can almost feel the vibrant quality of the religious experience of the writer and through him of the Christian community of which he is a part. These Christians are going through troublesome times. They face excommunication. They endure the hatred of the world. They suffer persecution. Despite all this, there is a radiance to their faith which we are compelled to admire. "To whom shall we go? You have the words of eternal life" (6:68). The experiences of "freedom" (8:31–36), "peace" (14:27;16:33), "joy" (15:11; 16:20–24;17:13), and answered prayer (16:24) are all a part of the portrayal which comes to us through the message of the Evangelist. He can write about these things because he himself has experienced them. They open for us a window on this first-century Christian community. We are given a positive, optimistic, and affirming impression. No matter what tribulation they might need to endure, they were of "good cheer." Christ had overcome the world, and through him they were sharing in that victory (16:33).

R. Schnackenburg associates two main ideas with John's understanding of "believing." The first is the matter of confessing that Jesus is the Christ. The second builds on the first and involves obedience and discipleship. Christian character should be a natural corollary and consequence of faith. Schnackenburg writes:

> Johannine faith is intrinsically ordained to confessing; it is a faith to be expressed in Christological confessions, which must persevere in face of unbelief (in the Gospel) and heresy (in I John). . . .
>
> Finally, Johannine faith is most intimately connected with discipleship . . . an active faith which is exercised in deeds as

well as in words and which perseveres in fraternal charity
(13:34 f.; 15:8).[13]

Another helpful definition is the one given by Schlier in
which he ties together faith and knowledge. He writes:

Faith is the determined obedience of trusting and loving
knowledge (acknowledgement), which has responded to the
pull of grace.[14]

Since John uses the word "grace" only once but often speaks
of the love of God, perhaps the definition would be improved
by substituting the word "love" for "grace." It is clear,
however, that John understands faith to include knowledge
and obedience. This keeps it from being an abstract emo-
tional or intellectual commitment to Jesus. It is anchored in
life and transforms human values and behavior. If it does
not, then whatever it is, it is not faith as John understands it.

One of the finest brief yet comprehensive definitions of
believing as found in John is the one given by F. Mussner.
He defines believing in John as

the determined, complete and confident turning of the whole
person with all of his strength to Jesus.[15]

Perhaps no better summary of what John means by believing
could be given. We should understand by this, of course, that
Jesus is here viewed as God's messenger. Therefore, in
turning to him, the believer is through him turning to God the
Father, who sent him into the world to be its Savior.

7

~~~~~~

Know

In The Gospel According to John eternal life is described as "knowing" God and "knowing" Jesus Christ, whom God has sent into the world (17:3). John uses two different Greek verbs to express the idea of knowing, but he completely avoids the noun *gnōsis,* meaning "knowledge." Two reasons have been suggested for this unusual feature of the Fourth Gospel. It may be that John is reacting to what in his view is an improper use of *gnōsis* among certain Christian groups at the time he is writing. The word *gnōsis* may already have had "resonances that were suspect." [1] Another possibility is that his avoidance of the noun stems from the author's understanding of Christian knowledge. It was for him more than a series of dogmas or doctrines that were to be learned; it was a life that was to be experienced. As one author put it, John's reluctance to use the noun "is perhaps due to a certain dynamic quality, a kind of vivacity in the Johannine conception of religion." [2] It is possible that both factors had a part to play in John's preference for the verbal forms.

John uses the two words for "to know" much more

extensively than do the other Gospel writers as the following table readily demonstrates:

	Matt.	Mark	Luke	John	I John
ginōskein ("to know")	20	13	28	56	25
eidenai ("to know")	25	23	26	85	15

Some interpreters have attempted to find a clear distinction in John's use of these two verbs. The first is said to mean "to acquire knowledge," or "to know by experience," or "to understand." The second word, *eidenai*, is taken to mean the possession of definite knowledge about something without any emphasis upon having learned it. It means to know in an absolute sense.[3] While instances can be cited where this distinction can be maintained, on other occasions John uses the words quite synonymously and without discrimination. It is best, therefore, to treat the variation as of no great significance and to regard them as synonyms.[4] It is a characteristic of John's writing style to introduce slight variations in his vocabulary without intending thereby a subtle shift in meaning.

In ordinary Greek usage, knowledge denotes the intelligent grasp of an object or situation.[5] Knowledge was viewed as a kind of seeing.[6] In the Fourth Gospel the verb *ginōskein* ("to know") is found side by side with verbs for seeing. Examples would be:

If you had known me, you would have known my Father also; henceforth you know him and have seen him. (14:7)

He will give you another Counselor, . . . whom the world cannot receive, because it neither sees him nor knows him. (14:16–17)

The same tendency to place "knowing" parallel to "seeing" can be noted in I John, where we read,

> No one who abides in him sins; no one who sins has either seen him or known him. (I John 3:6)

The juxtaposition of these words suggests that the author shares in some measure the Greek idea of "knowing." At the same time, a deeper study of John's view of knowledge soon indicates that he includes in it ideas that go beyond Greek connotations. P. Bonnard[7] finds four different meanings for knowledge in John. The first two, namely, "to know a fact" and "to understand," would be fully in keeping with Greek ideas. John also uses knowing in two other senses, namely, as a word closely tied to believing and finally as the equivalent to personal fellowship or communion. Here John shows Hebraic rather than Greek influence.

In the Old Testament the knowledge of God centered in communion, fellowship, and obedience rather than in knowledge "about God." [8] Facts and doctrine were not primary. Rather, the ideas of commitment and obedience dominated. We are told, for example, that the sons of Eli were worthless men; "they knew not the LORD" (I Sam. 2:12, KJV), that is, "they had no regard for the LORD"(RSV). This meant that they did not reverence and obey God. Instead, they were rebellious and disobedient. It was not a lack of factual or doctrinal knowledge which led to their condemnation by the writer but an attitude of life which showed a total disregard for the laws of Israel. Their lives were characterized by arrogant independence and moral excesses.

Another illustration of the use of "knowledge" in the Old Testament can be seen in the following example of Hebrew poetry where the second line parallels the first in meaning:

> O continue thy steadfast love to those who know thee,
> and thy salvation to the upright of heart!
>
> (Ps. 36:10)

For the psalmist, "knowing God" was synonymous with "being upright in heart." The expression has moral and ethical overtones and implies living in accordance with the will of God. Elsewhere it is implied that "knowing the Lord" can be equated with having the law of God written "within," that is, written "upon the heart." [9] This means to do God's will voluntarily and gladly rather than in response to external demand or coercion.

What is distinctive about the Hebrew connotation of "knowledge" is its experiential quality. "Knowing" involves more than the intellect. When used in a religious context it carries the connotations of obedience, righteousness, and fellowship. Such ideas are not a part of normal Greek usage. John attaches to his words for "knowing" meanings that have been derived from the corresponding Hebrew words. For John, knowledge and obedience are one. [10]

Believing and knowing. On rare occasions John distinguishes between believing and knowing. An example of such distinction would be John's teaching concerning the mutual relationship and indwelling of the Father and the Son. This is expressed in John only in terms of "knowing," never of "believing." Normally, however, the two words are used in a way which suggests that the meanings overlap with one another. In some instances, when the two words appear together believing is placed before knowing, as in the following passage:

And we have believed, and have come to know, that you are the Holy One of God. (6:69)

In other cases the order of the verbs is reversed, as in 16:30 and 17:8. This also occurs in I John, where we read, "So we know and believe the love God has for us" (I John 4:16). Bultmann's comment here is helpful:

> Faith and knowledge do not differ as to their substance. . . .
> No, faith is everything. Knowledge cannot cut loose from
> faith and soar on out beyond it. . . . Knowing is a structural
> aspect of believing.[11]

Knowing Jesus the Christ. An important insight into John's
distinctive message about the knowledge of God comes from
the following statement:

> And this is eternal life, that they know thee the only true God,
> and Jesus Christ whom thou hast sent. (17:3)

John goes beyond the message of Judaism here by linking the
knowledge of Jesus Christ with the knowledge of God. For
John, the only valid knowledge of God comes through Jesus
Christ, who alone reveals the Father and who is the one
mediator between God and man. Only through him can life
be found. Jesus, not Moses, is the ultimate revealer of the
Father.

The knowledge of God spoken of in 17:3 implies an
intimate relationship of fellowship and love (cf. I John 1:2–3).
Herein lies the very essence of the life of the believer.

Union with God. The concept of the knowledge of God in
John carries with it the idea of union with God. John does
not distinguish between union with God and union with Jesus
Christ. He writes:

> I . . . pray that they may all be one; even as thou, Father, art
> in me, and I in thee, that they also may be in us, so that the
> world may believe that thou hast sent me. (17:20–21)

This does not mean absorption or loss of identity, but it is the
author's way of expressing the reality of the intimate fellowship that exists or should exist between the believer and God.
Dodd comments that for the prophets of the Old Testament
the height of religious knowledge was to apprehend in
experience the unique majesty of God as Lord. He adds that

for John this experience is made possible through the recognition of Christ as the revelation of God, of Christ as inseparably one with God; and it finds its completion in an experience of our unity with Christ in God.[12]

This new relationship and experience of unity is also a relationship of mutual love.[13]

John and Gnosticism. In reexpressing the Gospel in terms of "knowledge," the author of the Gospel of John differs considerably from the accounts found in the Synoptics. In the Fourth Gospel we have a vocabulary that bears a resemblance to later Gnostic terminology.[14] Similarity of vocabulary need not imply that John's ideas are basically "Gnostic." It appears that while John uses religious vocabulary which is current in his day, he uses it for his own ends. The content of what he writes is his own. The form in which he expresses it appears to be sensitive to contemporary trends and vocabulary. Perhaps he uses the language of current religious thought in order to build a bridge to some of his readers who have been exposed to incipient Gnostic thought.[15]

Gnosticism is a movement about which much new information has come to light. Until very recently Gnosticism was known chiefly through the polemical writings of early church fathers, especially Irenaeus and Hippolytus. The discovery in 1946 of the Nag Hammadi Coptic texts at Chenoboskion in Upper Egypt has made available for the first time many of the actual writings of the Gnostics. These Coptic documents are dated from the third and fourth centuries A.D. and are considered to be translations of Greek originals coming from the second century A.D.[16] The chief value of the Nag Hammadi documents is the direct testimony they give of Gnostic doctrines. Instead of being dependent upon a number of secondary witnesses and a few late products of the movement, we now have the actual writings of the Gnostics.

To use the designation "Gnosticism" as if it were a clearly identifiable system of thought is somewhat misleading. This is particularly true in the early stages of the movement. Some helpful distinctions have been suggested by R. McL. Wilson,[17] who distinguishes three successive stages in the movement. These are:

1. The precursors of Gnosticism as exemplified by Philo and possibly the Essenes of the Dead Sea Scrolls.

2. The Gnosticism opposed by Irenaeus and Hippolytus, which came into full flourish in the second century A.D., and also the pagan Gnosticism of the *Hermetica*, an extensive group of writings current in the second and third centuries and produced in Egypt. The Hermetica derive their name from the god Hermes, or Thoth, the god of wisdom, who was supposedly the source of the revelation contained in these Greek tractates.

3. The systems of Manichaeism and Mandaeism, from the third century A.D. and later.

The element common to all Gnostic systems which has given them their name is the theme of *gnōsis* ("knowledge"). Before the coming of Christianity many of the features that were later gathered into Gnostic systems were present but seem not to have been grouped together into an identifiable philosophy. Christianity appears to have acted as a catalyst to bring about a systematizing of Gnostic elements within a quasi-Christian framework.

C. H. Dodd[18] summarizes well our present state of knowledge regarding Gnosticism as follows:

> 1. There is no Gnostic document known to us which can with any show of probability be dated—at any rate in the form of which alone we have access to it—before the period of the New Testament.
>
> 2. The typical Gnostic systems all combine in various ways and proportions ideas derived from Christianity with ideas

which can be shown to be derived from, or at least to have affinities with, other religious or philosophical traditions. 3. The various Gnostic systems differ widely in the way in which they introduce and combine these disparate elements.

While Dodd appears to be correct in saying that we do not possess Gnostic documents that antedate Christianity, this does not rule out the fact that we do possess manuscripts which contain emphases that can be called "proto-Gnostic," as, for example, documents such as the Dead Sea Scrolls, which stress "knowledge" and dualism, from a time earlier than Christianity. This is what Wilson appears to have in mind when he designates these as "the precursors of Gnosticism." Wilson prefers to speak of this material as "pre-Gnosis" rather than as "pre-Christian Gnosticism." [19]

Gnosticism, even when the term is limited to Wilson's second category, that is, the type of systems that were rejected by Irenaeus and Hippolytus, cannot be lumped together and viewed as a unity. Gnosticism is a moving, developing system with many branches. The following characteristics are generally found in all of them. They teach a physical dualism in which it is held that a great chasm exists between the material world (of which men are a part) and a higher order or spiritual world. This higher order is not known by the natural man. Even the Greek philosophers could not attain this knowledge. Such knowledge is not attained by study or by self-effort. It is mystically communicated, and only a few, that is, "the Gnostics," attain it. Those other Christians who do not achieve this special *gnōsis* possess only "faith" rather than "knowledge." This is regarded as an inferior stage of religious development.

The special knowledge claimed by the Gnostics involves an explanation of the origin of the universe and of man. A recurring expression of the Gnostics was the phrase, "I know myself and I know whence I am." The particular forms of

Gnosticism attacked by Irenaeus taught that there were many mediators between God and man. These mediators were called aeons and they were thirty in number. These systems also held to what was called a Demiurge. This was the God of the Old Testament and the God of creation. He is different from the real God. The purpose of the Demiurge in the Gnostic system was to keep the true God removed from matter which was viewed as inherently evil. God who is good could not have created that which is evil. Here the dualism of Gnosticism comes into sharp focus.

In the Gnostic systems attacked by Irenaeus "the distinctive truths of Christianity were swamped in alien speculations," to use the words of C. H. Dodd.[20] In these systems there was a denial of the incarnation, the substitution of many mediators for one mediator, Jesus Christ, the separation of God from matter to such an extent that the creation is attributed to someone else, the claim that these systems possessed secret formulas of power whereby the initiate could mount successfully from the lower realm of the present world, where he does not really belong, to the higher realm of the spirit. One of the outstanding characteristics of the Gnostics was the claim that each Gnostic had a direct, personal, ecstatic vision of God. While John also speaks of "knowing" God and of "seeing" him, it is not the kind of vision the Gnostics had in mind. It is not in John a secret, ineffable experience. Rather, *Jesus* is the revelation of God. It is by responding to him, through believing, that a person "sees" God and receives life. As R. Schnackenburg writes:

> The Christian message is not just a variant of Gnostic thought. . . . It is something entirely different and new. . . . The "scandal" of the incarnation . . . signals a way of redemption utterly foreign to that of Gnosis.[21]

Schnackenburg[22] noted four ways in which Johannine knowledge of God differs from that of Gnosticism:

1. In John knowledge is not concerned with "self-knowledge" but with a genuine knowledge of God which leads to communion with God.

2. This knowledge of God is dependent upon a divine revelation and is essentially different from any Gnostic "revelation." The Christian believes in a revelation which took place in an historical event and which has become the subject of proclamation for the whole world. This revelation the Christian receives neither through initiation nor through an ecstatic trance but through hearing the gospel in faith.

3. Jesus is the mediator of salvation. His coming is anchored in history and not in a mythical, nonhistorical revelation, as it is in Gnosticism.

4. Whoever would know God must keep his commandments. This concern of John is not found in Gnosticism. The latter is concerned with escape *from* this world, not with an ethical way of life *in* this world.

Another distinction is pointed out by C. K. Barrett[23] when he writes that for John man's wretchedness is due not to ignorance but to sin. It might be added that in John sin is primarily unbelief. His central doctrine is that Jesus is the Christ and that God has revealed himself in him. Rather than stressing esoteric mysteries, as Gnosticism does, John has a message he proclaims to all men everywhere. As R. P. Casey has written,

> The Christ of the Fourth Gospel is essentially a revealer and the elect are distinguished by their knowledge and acceptance of Christian doctrine.[24]

From the many differences that have been noted it would be correct to say that a wide chasm divides The Gospel According to John from the developed Gnostic systems of the second century. While there are certain verbal similarities to Gnosticism, the essence of John's message differs radically from that found in Gnosticism. John reflects an awareness of

movements that were current in his day which expressed
salvation in terms of knowledge, and his own vocabulary
appears to have been colored by that awareness.

Suggestions have been made that it is in Wilson's first
category, which he termed "pre-Gnosis," rather than in
second-century Gnosticism that influences on John should be
sought. It is in this connection that Floyd V. Filson wrote:

> I would not use the term "Gnostic" of the climate in which the
> Christian message took form. But I would not object to using
> the term "pre-Gnostic." [25]

This *gnōsis* terminology need not be viewed as derived from
pagan sources. It is present to a considerable degree in the
Dead Sea Scrolls materials. John appears to have been
written and shaped, at least in part, by interaction between a
Christian community and a hostile Jewish community.

Knowledge in the Qumran literature. The possession of
"knowledge," "wisdom," and "truth" is a repeated theme in
the writings of Qumran. The frequency of the references to
knowledge gives to this theme an unusual prominence. Four
aspects of the knowledge of Qumran stand out:[26]

1. The knowledge which they possess is held to be revealed
to them by God.

2. It is an esoteric knowledge which is not to be shared
with those outside the fellowship.

3. The knowledge that they possess involves a proper
understanding of the law of Moses and an ardent desire and
effort on their part to conform their lives to their unique
interpretation of the law.

4. There are also passages which indicate that the sect
thought of itself as the faithful in Israel who were preparing in
the desert a highway for the messianic age and the knowledge
they possessed involved special information concerning
events that would take place at this "end time" before the
new age dawned.

Comparison of the knowledge of Qumran with Gnosticism.
Compared with Gnosticism, there is in the concept of
knowledge in the scrolls a greater stress on law and ethics. It
is not that Gnosticism was devoid of ethics, but its strength
did not lie in that direction, whereas, as W. D. Davies
expressed it, "the Dead Sea Sect reveals ethical passion." [27]
  Both the Qumran literature and Gnosticism stress the
esoteric aspect of the knowledge which they claim to possess.
For both, it is a revealed knowledge. The differences lie both
in the manner of revelation and in the content. It is not
through dreams and trances but through chosen leaders that
God has shared his secrets with the community. Whereas
Gnosticism was concerned with self-knowledge and specula
tions about the creation of the world and the destiny of man
the writers of Qumran focused on understanding and obeying
the law of God. They also claimed knowledge of the fact that
they were living in the day just before the new messianic age
would appear. They looked for a renewal of this world.
Gnosticism sought an escape *from* this world. The scrolls'
concept of knowing God is in harmony with the Old
Testament idea of obedience and communion. The Gnostic
concept of a special vision of God is not shared at Qumran.
  Because of the marked differences between the ideas of
Qumran and those of Gnosticism it is clear that the term
"Gnosticism" should not be applied to the Dead Sea Scrolls.[28]
It is much better to speak of this as "pre-Gnosis," or a similar
expression. F. F. Bruce has written:

> We shall look in vain for that *gnosis* which enables the soul to
> liberate itself progressively from its imprisonment in matter by
> ascending through the spheres to the upper realm of spirit.
> The knowledge cultivated at Qumran was the knowledge
> recommended in the Old Testament Wisdom books, which
> finds its source in the fear of God.[29]

Comparison of the knowledge of Qumran, Gnosticism, and

John. While the scrolls stress a revelational, esoteric, eschatological, and legal knowledge with great stress on ethics and obedience to the commandments of God, the Fourth Gospel's concept of knowledge centers in a communion or fellowship with God through Jesus Christ. The legalism, ethics, eschatological views, and secrecy element are not a part of the Fourth Gospel's teaching on knowledge.

Earlier we noted how John also differs from Gnosticism. While there are similarities in terminology, the elaborate cosmology of this literature, the secret formulas, the ecstatic vision, and the result of becoming like God, which are emphases of these writings, are not repeated in John. John's concept of knowledge, insofar as it reflects Old Testament and especially Wisdom literature, is closer to Qumran than to Gnosticism. In terminology, however, his writings bear a close resemblance to Gnosticism. By choosing the vocabulary that he did choose, the author of the Fourth Gospel appears to have been reacting to certain ideas that were current in the religious atmosphere of his time. This was not full-blown Gnosticism, but it contained ideas that were subsequently absorbed into second-century Gnosticism. I John clearly contains a polemic against a number of ideas that later came to full expression in Gnosticism. In the Fourth Gospel there also appears to be a polemic against what we may call "pre-Gnosis" or "incipient Gnosticism," but it is not so clearly or forcefully expressed as in the case of the First Letter. It was perhaps for this reason that second-century Gnostics found John somewhat congenial to their thought and interpreted it in such a way as to make it supportive of some of their sectarian doctrines.[30]

Conclusion. A study of the Dead Sea Scrolls and of Gnosticism helps to give insight into the religious ideas that were current or were in formation at the time the Fourth Gospel was written. As we have noted, John bears some resemblances to both these literatures and his vocabulary indicates awareness of the religious vocabulary that was current at the time of writing. John, however, has his own message and he gives his own connotations to the words he uses even when he shares a common vocabulary with other religious movements. For him salvation means "knowing" God and Jesus Christ whom he has sent. Such knowledge implies commitment, love, fellowship, and obedience. It is made possible through Jesus Christ, who alone knows the Father and has made him known among men. Jesus is the one mediator between God and man. Believing and knowing, while occasionally distinguished in John, are closely interrelated and at times appear to be used quite synonymously.

8

~~~~~~

Love

Love plays such a central role in the thought of the Fourth Gospel that the author has been called the apostle of love. The following list indicates the relative frequency with which the two words for love are found in the four Gospels. Their use in I John is also included.

	Matt.	Mark	Luke	John	I John
agapē ("love"), and					
agapan ("to love")	9	6	14	44	46
philein ("to love")	5	1	2	13	0

Clearly, love has become an overriding concern in the Johannine community. The Fourth Gospel lacks anything comparable to the Sermon on the Mount with its ethical instructions. For the author of John, love has become the

118

essence of Christian ethical instruction. It is the norm for judging Christian character.

The new commandment. Love is called the new commandment. It is given twice in the farewell discourses.

A new commandment I give to you, that you love one another; even as I have loved you, that you also love one another. (13:34)

This is my commandment, that you love one another as I have loved you. . . . This I command you, to love one another. (15.12,17)

What is "new" about this commandment? This question is answered very well by V. P. Furnish, who writes:

The commandment is called "new" because it is brought by the one in whom the new age has been instituted.[1]

"The new factor," says G. Schrenk, "is its new christological foundation."[2] In the other Gospels it is at this point that Jesus institutes the Lord's Supper with the words,

This cup which is poured out for you is the new *(kainē)* covenant in my blood. (Luke 22:20)

The repetition of the adjective "new" is very significant here. There seems to be a definite connection between the "new commandment" and the "new covenant." The "old covenant"—that is, the covenant under Moses—and its demands were spoken of as "the commandment." Paul does this in the following passage in which he appears to refer to the time when as a Jewish boy he came "of age" and was now judged to be personally responsible for his actions under the Jewish law:

I was once alive apart from the law, but when the commandment came, sin revived and I died; the very commandment which promised life proved to be death to me. (Rom. 7:9–10)

"The commandment" was an expression used by the Jews to refer to the ten commandments, to the law of Moses. The giving of the covenant and the giving of the ten commandments go hand in hand. The commandments were the basis of the covenant. Hence covenant and commandment are intimately interrelated. So also in John. This has led one writer to state:

> I conclude that the *entole kaine* (new commandment) of which the Lord speaks *is* the *kaine diatheke* (new covenant). . . . The covenant is an act of grace. God in His goodness promises to dispense His mercies, but requires a definite response from man. A commandment is therefore necessarily inherent in a covenant of grace.[3]

This interpretation is supported by Raymond E. Brown, who writes,

> The newness of the commandment of love is really related to the theme of covenant at the Last Supper—the "new commandment" of John 13:34 is the basic stipulation of the "new covenant" of Luke 22:20.[4]

It should be remembered that it is not only the new covenant that is intimately related to love. This is true also of the covenant that God made with Israel through Moses. God chose this people and revealed himself to them. They did not deserve God's love. This is the repeated message of the Old Testament. G. Quell speaks of this tie between the old covenant and love in these words:

> There can be no doubt that the thought of the covenant is itself an expression in juridical terms of the experience of the love of God. Hence the concept of love is the ultimate foundation of the whole covenant theory.[5]

What is distinctive about the New Covenant is the death of Jesus for the world. God so loved the world that he gave his Son (3:16).

The meaning of love. In pre-Biblical Greek three verbs are used to express love: *eran, philein,* and *agapan. Eran* is "passionate love which desires others for itself." [6] *Philein* speaks of the love of friend for friend. *Agapan* lacks the sensuous quality of *eran* and the warmth of *philein.* E. Evans interprets the verb to mean primarily "approval" and speaks of it involving a deliberate act of the will. *Philein,* he argues, is a stronger term and means "a positive devotion." He writes:

> I think it is now clear that *agapan* signifies not a feeling or an emotion, but a deliberate act of the will; and further, that as the word originally implied the approval of the less by the greater, this sense also survives.[7]

The Gospel According to John and I John use only *philein* and *agapan.* Gradually the distinction between these two words became somewhat blurred in classical Greek and they appear to have been used increasingly as synonyms.[8] The Septuagint was very influential in enriching the meaning of *agapan* through its choice of this verb to translate the Hebrew verb "to love," *'aheb.* The colorless Greek word began to take on the rich nuances of the Hebrew understanding of love, including God's love for Israel as expressed in the covenant and God's demand for the total love and allegiance of Israel in return.[9]

John never uses the noun *philia,* which corresponds to the verb *philein.* The noun *agapē,* corresponding to *agapan,* occurs seven times in the Gospel and eighteen times in I John. C. Spicq has given a fine description of the meaning of *agapē* in the Fourth Gospel. He writes:

> No text of Scripture tells more about charity than John 3:16 which reveals love as an attribute of the Father. Love is eternal because it exists before the sending of the Son; it inspires the plan of salvation. It is universal because it is for the whole world. It is completely gratuitous, with no motive

other than itself. It is gentle and merciful, active and powerful. In its desire to prove itself, it seizes the initiative. The fact of God's love most clearly revealed in the text is its immensity.[10]

Love, for John, when demanded of the disciples involves more than emotion. It implies obedience, for this is how love for God is demonstrated. We read:

> He who has my commandments and keeps them, he it is who loves me; and he who loves me will be loved by my Father, and I will love him and manifest myself to him. (14:21)

> If a man loves me, he will keep my word. (14:23)

The need for love to be demonstrated in action is emphasized also in I John 3:17–18. In this case the theme is love for one's brother.

The distinction between *agapan* and *philein*, which was present in pre-Biblical Greek, appears not to be observed in the body of The Gospel According to John. They seem to be used interchangeably and synonymously. The following examples indicate that this is the case:

1. The Father's love for the Son is expressed in 3:35 by *agapan* and in 5:20 by *philein.*

2. Jesus' love for Lazarus is expressed in 11:3 by *philein* and in 11:5 by *agapan.*

3. Jesus' love for the beloved disciple is expressed in 13:23 by *agapan* and in 20:2 by *philein.*

4. The Father's love for the disciples (because they love Jesus) is expressed in 14:23 by *agapan* and in 16:27 by *philein.*

5. Men's love for things which they place before God is expressed in 3:19 by *agapan* and in 12:25 by *philein.*

Some have interpreted the interchange between Peter and Jesus in the Epilogue (21:15–17) as suggesting a distinction in meaning between *agapan* and *philein.* Jesus asks Peter if he loves *(agapan)* him; Peter says he does love him, using *philein.*

The second question and response are identical to the first. The third time Jesus changes verbs and says, "Do you love me?" *(philein).* Then the text states,

Peter was grieved because he said to him the third time *(to triton),* "Do you love me? *(philein)"*

Some have suggested that Peter used *philein* because he did not believe he could measure up to the higher love implied by *agapan.*[11] E. Evans makes the distinction in the opposite direction, making Jesus mean by the question in which he uses *agapan:* "Are you satisfied with me now? You are not disappointed in me anymore, are you?"[12] Peter's reply in which he uses *philein* is interpreted to mean, "Even more than that, thou knowest, I have a positive devotion to you, as you very well know." Peter is then said to be unhappy that it is not until the third time that Jesus is willing to use the stronger of the two words.

This builds too much on a distinction that goes back to non-Biblical usage. John elsewhere in the Gospel treats the words synonymously. He does the same with other words when for variety he alternates between synonyms. An example would be his word for "knowing": he uses quite freely both *oida* and *ginōskein* with no apparent distinction intended. Leon Morris' comment is to the point:

He [Hendriksen] fails to notice that it is John's habit to introduce slight variations in repetitions and this makes his argument less cogent. We may well agree that, while the two verbs are of very similar meaning, there is yet a distinction on occasion. But it does not follow that a writer who elsewhere shows himself prone to slight variations, including the use of synonyms, without appreciable difference of meaning, does intend a difference of meaning here.[13]

Bultmann simply comments:

The exchange of *agapan* and *philein* cannot be significant, for in the third question Jesus also uses *philein* instead of *agapan.*[14]

A helpful translation, which brings out clearly that Jesus is asking the *same* question each time, is that found in the New English Bible, which reads:

> A third time he said, "Simon son of John, do you love me?"
> (21:17)

This does not mean that on the third occasion he asked a new question. The expression "a third time" implies that Jesus is *repeating* the question he had asked on the previous two occasions.

Universal love versus particular love. E. Käsemann has properly pointed out that the concept of love in the Fourth Gospel is not without problems. He writes:

> It is not . . . universally recognized that John demands love for one's brethren, but not for one's enemies, and correspondingly that Jesus loves his own, but not the world. . . . There is no indication in John that love for one's brother would also include love towards one's neighbor, as demanded in other books of the New Testament. On the contrary, John here sets forth an unmistakable restriction such as we also know from the Qumran community, and this also indicates the historical situation of our Gospel with unusual clarity.[15]

On the matter of love we seem to have in the Gospel of John a union of opposites. There is in this Gospel, at one and the same time, a perspective that embraces the whole world and alongside of this the new commandment given by Jesus to his disciples that they "love one another." Concerning God it is heralded that he loves the world (3:16–17); but to the believers it is commanded that they love one another (13:34; 15:12,17). The first love is universal; the second, particular. The first is inclusive; the second, exclusive. The disciples are commanded to love one another as Jesus has loved them (15:12). They are not commanded to love the world as God loved the world. The love that they are enjoined to have is a more restricted love, limited to those who have responded affirmatively to the proclamation that Jesus is the Christ, the Son of God. As a result, in this Gospel the broader concern for the world stands side by side with the more narrow imperative to love the brethren.

What are the reasons for this contrasting emphasis? Does a real tension exist here between two opposite tendencies? Does the writer have multiple purposes in mind which help to account for the juxtaposition of the universal and particular in this way in his Gospel?

One way to remove the tension is to take away one of the opposites. The universal interpretation of John 3:16 is removed by Käsemann, who says that this does not represent the writer's own viewpoint. Käsemann argues:

> We have every reason to consider this verse as a traditional primitive Christian formula which the Evangelist employed.[16]

The difficulty with this explanation is that the universal concern of the Fourth Gospel is widely expressed in the book and is by no means confined to this verse.

Another suggestion that has been made is to limit the meaning of the phrase "God so loved the world" to mean only "his own" in the world and not all men. This interpretation is expressed in these words:

> We cannot press *kosmos* here to mean the *whole* cosmos, good and evil elements alike. The divine love was set upon those "in the world" who were "his own"—those who, when the Light shone, saw it and came to it—those who did, as a matter of fact, "believe in him" and "receive everlasting life." What of those who did not believe, and "perished"? There is no hint that God loved them and yearned over them; they were simply not *his*. . . . The divine love for the world must be understood with this sharp dichotomy in mind.[17]

However, the word *kosmos* cannot here be made to mean

only the good elements in the world and then later mean the bad elements in the world as in 12:31; 14:17, and 15:18–19. It is better to regard this term as referring here to humanity in general—in other words, as having a neutral connotation. Other uses of this term suggest the same positive attitude to the world which is found in 3:16. These are:

> For the bread of God is that which comes down from heaven, and gives life to the world. (6:33)

> I did not come to judge the world but to save the world. (12:47)

The universal. The cosmic and universal perspective of the Gospel of John can be seen in a number of places. It is said of the true light that it "enlightens *every* man" (1:9). This does not mean that all men gladly receive and embrace this light, for some men are willfully blind (9:39) and, although the light has come into the world, some love darkness rather than light, because their deeds are evil (3:19). The focus is on the fact that God gives light to all persons through the Christ. It may or may not be received. God's concern is for all, however, not just for some.

In John, ch. 4, there is a portrayal of a mission of Jesus to the Samaritans. This chapter appears to reflect the missionary concern of the Johannine community, or at least that of the writer, who wishes his readers to embrace the task of missionary outreach. The main lesson of the story is expressed by the words of Jesus when he tells his disciples that the Samaritan fields "are already white for harvest" (4:35). This concept of outreach and mission is reinforced when the villagers themselves say:

> We have heard for ourselves, and we know that this is indeed *the Savior of the world.* (4:42)

John's message is that the exclusivism of Judaism is broken.

Even Samaritans could be included in the new people of
God! Henceforth, neither Jerusalem nor Mt. Gerizim would
be the place of worship. "God is spirit, and those who
worship him must worship in spirit and truth" (4:24).
Provincialism and sectarianism have been transcended, because God's concern reaches out to all people everywhere.

The world mission as portrayed by John is seen further in
the discussion concerning the good Shepherd when Jesus
speaks of "other sheep" which must be brought into the fold
(10:16). It is also suggested by such a passage as the
following:

> Behold, the Lamb of God, who takes away the sin of the
> world! (1:29)

The mission was to all. It is reiterated in the statement:

> For God sent the Son into the world, not to condemn the
> world, but that the world might be saved through him. (3:17)

A final example is the promise of Jesus:

> And I, when I am lifted up from the earth, will draw *all men* to
> myself. (12:32)

Alongside this universal concern there emerges the command
to love within the brotherhood. This will be examined next.

The particular. Having stated that God loves the world,
John affirms that Jesus had a special love for his disciples:

> Having loved his own who were in the world, he loved them to
> the end. (13:1)

In the farewell discourses Jesus commands that they love
one another (13:34; 15:12,17). While W. F. Howard seeks to
defend the author against the charge of provincialism, he
does acknowledge that,

> There are places where we feel that St. John is limiting his
> outlook to the narrow circle of the Christian brotherhood,

with some indifference to the wider claims of society as a whole.[18]

Some years ago Paul Wernle expressed disappointment at what he called the "un-Christian" emphasis which he felt he detected in the Johannine literature. He wrote:

Unfortunately the Gnostic controversy introduced a hostile and censorious spirit into the Church itself, and so brotherly love was restricted to orthodox believers. . . . "Not for the world do I pray," says Jesus in the high-priestly prayer. And how poor a thing after all is the new commandment of love to each other—i.e., of Christian to Christians—compared with the absolute boundless love enjoined in the Sermon on the Mount. As the Gospel of St. John limits the frontiers of love in the direction of the world with a downright narrow-mindedness, so do the epistles against the heretics within the Church.[19]

How do we account for the presence in the Fourth Gospel of an affirmation of the universal love of God for the world while the command to the Christian disciple remains restricted? Why is there not a similarity between the two, with the command to the disciples including an exhortation to follow God's example of universal love? Where is the love for neighbor as expressed, for example, in the parable of the good Samaritan (Luke 10:29–37)?

Evangelism and instruction. Perhaps the reason these two loves (the one universal and the other particular) remain separate in the Fourth Gospel is directly related to the history behind the composition of this Gospel and to the aims which the author had in mind when he wrote. His purpose appears to have been twofold and to have included both evangelism and instruction.

We may well think of the first twelve chapters of John as

containing the *kērygma* (proclamation of the good news concerning Jesus Christ) of the Johannine church. In these chapters, after the formal opening of the Prologue, two basic elements are incorporated, namely, miracles and discourses. The miracles are called "signs" and each one reveals who Jesus is and is intended to lead men to believe in Jesus as the Christ. The discourses also center on Christology and on finding "life" through believing. These discourses often move from dialogue to monologue. They are a means for presenting the teachings of Jesus in Johannine terms. Frequently the only role played by the other person in the dialogue is to make brief comments, indicating some lack of understanding, or to ask questions. In either case this gives the opportunity for the instruction to be continued. In some instances the discourses become heated disputations, as is the case in the conversations between Jesus and "the Jews" in chs. 7 and 8. Sharp, bitter retorts are made on both sides. The opposition, spoken of as "the Jews," appears to include two groups. John uses the term "the Jews" in a technical sense to refer to official religious Judaism as represented by the hierarchy at Jerusalem. He also seems to have in mind the counterparts of these men as represented by leaders of the Jewish synagogues with whom, at the time of writing, the Johannine community was in intense and even acrimonious debate.

In viewing chs. 1 to 12 as containing Johannine *kerygma* and as having material that can properly be called evangelistic, we do not intend to suggest that these chapters were written or were originally circulated for the purpose of direct evangelism through the written word. The Gospel appears, rather, to have been written to instruct and encourage Christians living in the middle of an alien culture and in an atmosphere of religious controversy. The problems with which his readers are wrestling has prompted the author to include in his Gospel material that would strengthen their own faith and would aid them in the defense of their beliefs against the theological objections raised by representatives of Judaism.

It must be remembered that the early church did not separate *kērygma* and *didachē* into two distinct categories, as has been done in recent years for the sake of analysis. We do so merely for convenience and in order to show where the stress lies, whether on evangelism or on instruction. That the writer has commitment to Jesus as the Christ very much in mind in the Book of Signs is supported by the manner in which he brings this section of The Gospel According to John to a close. He concludes it with a final appeal for discipleship accompanied by a promise of life to those who believe and a warning of judgment to those who do not (12:44–50).

The instructional elements of The Gospel According to John are primarily concentrated in chs. 13 to 21. In this section of the Gospel we have the farewell discourses which include such elements as the exhortation to humble service (13:14–15), the command to love the brethren (13:34; 15:12,17), the promise of the Holy Spirit (14:16–26; 15:26; 16:7–16), the instruction to abide in the vine in order to bear fruit (15:4), encouragement in the face of persecution (15:18 to 16:4), the commission to be witnesses (15:27), the gift of peace (14:27; 16:33), and the prayer for unity (17:11,21).

In view of the fact that John's whole account of the passion of Jesus is theologically oriented, with each event being either a fulfillment of prophecy or in some way contributing to the revelation of the glory of Jesus, we should consider chs. 18 to 20 as also a part of John's theological instruction. These chapters interpret the meaning of Jesus' death and include the resurrection of Jesus, the Great Commission (20:21), the giving of the Spirit (20:22), the task of proclaiming forgiveness in Jesus' name (20:23), and the model Christian confession as voiced by Thomas (20:28). The Epilogue continues to focus on instruction. Included are the theme of mission as portrayed by the effectiveness of fishing when Jesus' instructions are followed (21:3–14), the command to feed the sheep (21:15–17), the exhortation to follow Jesus (21:19–22), and the explanation of the death of the beloved disciple (21:21–23). We see, therefore, that chs. 13 to 21 are characterized by Christian instruction, or *didachē*. Beginning with ch. 13, Jesus is with "his own" (13:1). At this point in the Gospel the focus shifts from the affirmation that Jesus is the Christ (or evangelism) to Christian discipleship.

Could it be that chs. 13 and following incorporate material that had previously existed as sermons proclaimed to the Johannine community? What had originally been presented as oral Christian teaching, which interpreted the meaning of Jesus to the Christian fellowship, was now assembled, modified, and molded into the document we know as The Gospel According to John.

We might think of the Gospel, then, as composed of two basic elements:

1. Chapters 1 to 12, which focus on *(a)* the miracles as "signs" in order to strengthen faith in Jesus as the Christ and which also include *(b)* a summary of current disputations between church and synagogue; and

2. Chapters 13 to 21 which in large measure comprise modified and expanded homilies formerly preached in the Johannine community.

In summary, the Fourth Gospel begins with a message for the world and concludes with instruction for the Christian church. The division in the Gospel stems from the author's selection from two kinds of source material that he had available. The proclamation of the love of God for the world was the message presented to both the Jewish and the Greek neighbors of the Johannine church. This *kērygma* stressed God's initiative in sending the Son to be the Savior of the world. These evangelistic messages were gathered and refined by the author and incorporated into his written Gospel. Since this good news met with opposition and led to disputations, these reactions are reflected in this part of John. Some of the issues that were debated are actually incorporated. The Jewish objections to the Christian claims concerning Jesus are faithfully mirrored. The author then presents counter arguments with which Christians endeavored to meet the Jewish theological opposition. Beginning with ch. 13 the author turns to the Christian *didachē* and concerns himself primarily with Christian doctrine and behavior.

It is because the two parts of John emerge from different life settings that they reflect a variance in emphasis. In his sharing the good news with the non-Christian community, the love of God for the world is stressed. In teaching the Christians, there is a shift to instruction in matters related to theology and conduct. In the author's mind there appears to have been no intended or conscious awareness of conflict between the universal love of God for the world and the particular love which the disciples were commanded to have toward one another. The two emphases simply reflect the two distinct milieus out of which The Gospel According to John developed. It must be admitted, however, that because of the "ingroup" perspective of chs. 13 to 21 the broader love of neighbor which both Judaism and Jesus taught does not find comparable expression in the Fourth Gospel. Here John's teachings need to be supplemented by the larger perspective found in the ethical instructions of Jesus as recorded in the Synoptic Gospels.

9

~~~~~~

Light and Darkness

John's Gospel tends to deal in antitheses and contrasts. This helps to give his presentation of the gospel a very dramatic quality. He places in opposition to each other life and death, light and darkness, freedom and bondage. These sharp antitheses are more than simply a literary characteristic of John's style of writing. They find their origin in John's religious perspective. A kind of religious dualism permeates the author's world view.

The two realms. The dualism John presents is not the Gnostic dualism which regards matter per se as evil and spirit as good. It involves, rather, a point of view which divides the universe into two distinct and opposing realms. This division of reality finds expression in John in a wide variety of terminology. One of the most characteristic and distinctive ways this is done is by the contrast between the realm which is "above" and that which is "below." Jesus says, for example,

> You are from below, I am from above; you are of this world, I am not of this world. (8:23)

When John speaks of the upper and lower worlds these worlds are, of course, not physically the one above the other. They are, however, morally and spiritually distinct. It is not a question of physical location but of spiritual values and allegiance.

In a certain sense, only Jesus is truly "from above." On the other hand, those who believe in Jesus as the Christ leave the realm of "the world" and move into God's realm. By their response to Jesus they demonstrate that God has chosen them "out of the world."

When Jesus entered this world he came "from above." He came down "from heaven" (3:13,31; 6:33–58). What does this mean? It means that Jesus has "come from God" (3:2). This is another way of saying that when Jesus speaks he does so with God's authority behind him. Jesus has come into this world with God's message and by his person and ministry reveals the Father. John sees Jesus as the spiritual link between heaven and earth. In John, Jesus says,

> Truly, truly, I say to you, you will see heaven opened, and the angels of God ascending and descending upon the Son of man. (1:51)

Concerning this passage, W. H. Cadman makes the following helpful observation:

> "Heaven lying open" means "God revealed." . . . The Son of Man may here be compared either with Jacob or with the ladder in the story of Bethel. In the one case, we are being told that it is now possible to see God . . . because Jesus, as Son of Man, is in continuous communication with God. If on the other hand the Son of Man is being compared with the ladder, then Jesus, as Son of Man, is the means of connexion between earth and heaven, the medium for bringing about continuous communication between man and God.[1]

Jesus is the mediator between God and man. He alone reveals the Father.

To Jesus, God the Father gave certain men who have been chosen "out of the world" (15:19; 17:6). Consequently they are not "of the world" (16:33; 17:16) even as Christ is not "of this world" (8:23). To be "of the world" is to be "from below." Consequently those who are "not of the world" are, by implication, like Jesus "from above."

John tells us how this transference from one realm or loyalty to another can take place. It is through what he terms a birth "from above" (3:3,7). Such a birth is through the ministration of the Spirit (3:8). That *anōthen* in 3:3,7 should be rendered "from above" is in keeping with the use of this word elsewhere in John (see 3:31; 19:11,23) even though Nicodemus misunderstands it as "again." Such misunderstanding is part of the literary technique of the author, who uses it to provide opportunity for a theme to be explained more fully by Jesus.

"Birth from above" or "of the Spirit" is necessary if a man is to "see" or "enter" the kingdom of God. John's use of the expression "kingdom of God" differs from that found in the Synoptic Gospels. There it refers to the rule or reign of God. In John it carries the added nuance of being the realm that is "above." It is, as Schnackenburg[2] has pointed out, the divine sphere. It is the heavenly realm to which Christ leads those who believe in him (12:26; 14:3; 17:24). To be chosen "out of the world" implies that these believers now properly belong to the realm that is "from above." Hence they are destined in the future to be "with Christ" to behold his glory which he had before the foundation of the world (17:24). While it is true that only the Christ "descended" from heaven (3:13), the implication of Jesus' prayer for his followers is that those who have believed in him are destined to share in his ascension into the presence of God the Father.

John has a number of other ways in which he expresses the religious dualism in which he understands reality. He speaks, for example, of the contrast between truth and falsehood

(8:44, 45; cf. I John 1:10; 2:4, 21, 22, 27; 4:20), and of that between freedom and bondage (8:31–36). To the above lists of opposites could be added a number of instances of an implied dualism. This is found in the promise of "living water" to meet man's thirst (4:10) and in the gift of "the true bread from heaven" to provide for man's spiritual hunger (6:32). In these instances, and in many others, Jesus is consistently portrayed as the one who has come to meet man's need however that need may be felt or expressed. The signs and discourses in John reflect a universal quality. They point beyond the local incidents that they describe to truths that are eternal and unrestricted to time or place. By this means the reader is constantly being encouraged to believe in Jesus as the Christ who can meet *his* particular need even though he stands more than a generation removed from Jesus when he lived on earth. By such personal commitment to Jesus the reader can move from the lower realm of the "world" into the higher realm of the "kingdom of God." In this way he can become a partaker of the benefits of the salvation which Jesus brings. By believing in Jesus he can have life in all its fullness (10:10).

The two realms in conflict. The present "world" is viewed by John as being under the control of the devil, who is called "the ruler of this world" (12:31–32; 14:30; 16:11). Those who reject Jesus reject the Father as well. Consequently they are said to belong to the devil and to be doing his works (8:42–44).

The bitter conflict in which the two realms are engaged is presented in such sharp contrasts as light and darkness and flesh and spirit:

The light shines in the darkness, and the darkness has not overcome it. (1:5)

It is the spirit that gives life, the flesh is of no avail. (6:63)

This hostility finds expression in personal hatred toward the believer. Jesus predicts:

> If the world hates you, know that it has hated me before it hated you. (15:18)

But along with this note of warning there is the reassuring affirmation of victory:

> In the world you have tribulation; but be of good cheer, I have overcome the world [literally, conquered] (16:33)

In an earlier chapter the dichotomy of life and death was discussed. By believing, one moves from death to life (5:21,24, 25; 8:51).

When the author contrasts flesh and spirit (1:13; 3:6; 6:63; 8:15–16) he does not have in mind the Gnostic dualism between body and spirit. He does not regard the body as a tomb of the soul.[3] Nor does he think of flesh as evil.[4] He does say that as far as the acquiring of salvation or "life" is concerned, the flesh can do nothing to earn or win it (6:63). Eternal life comes only through the Spirit. The Spirit of God lifts men from their natural level in the flesh to the level of the spirit. This is what is meant by birth "from above." Through this experience, man is raised from the lower to the upper world. The flesh is not thereby removed but is indwelt by the Spirit.[5] Another occurrence of the word "flesh" is in the expression,

> You judge according to the flesh, I judge no one. (8:15)

Jesus' opponents were judging according to the external appearance. They knew nothing of the higher world of the Spirit. Thus their judgment was a superficial judgment and a false one.

A frequent contrast in John and one that is often joined to that of life and death is the opposition of light and darkness as expressed above in 1:5. Other examples would be 3:19:

8:12; 9:5; 12:35,46. Note that the themes of light and darkness both end with the Book of Signs. In the farewell discourses Jesus is with his "own." Judas, who does not belong, soon leaves. When he leaves we are told that it "was night" (13:30). For John this statement probably had symbolic meaning, for elsewhere in the gospel he uses day and night as contrasts in much the same way that he opposes light to darkness. This motif appears in such passages as the following:

> We must work the works of him who sent me, while it is day; night comes, when no one can work. (9:4)

> Are there not twelve hours in the day? If any one walks in the day, he does not stumble, because he sees the light of this world. But if any one walks in the night, he stumbles, because the light is not in him. (11:9–10)

This motif is carried still farther in the extension of the idea into sight and blindness (9:39–41).

The meaning of the expression "the Jews" in the Fourth Gospel. In John "the Jews" are said to be "from below" (8:23). They are the representatives of darkness and are blind (9:39–40). What does John mean by this? Is he anti-Semitic? No, this is not for him an ethnic term. It must be recognized that in John the expression "the Jews" has become a technical one. It refers not to the people at large but to the hierarchy of Judaism with its headquarters at Jerusalem. They represent the official opposition to Jesus. They are consistently referred to in John in a polemical tone. As the author writes, he appears to have in mind not only the hierarchy of Jerusalem in Jesus' day but also the Jewish religious rulers of his own time and place. These are the logical descendants of the earlier hierarchy, and at the time of writing they are the ones who oppose the Christians and who refuse to accept the Christian claim that Jesus is the Christ.

John seeks constantly to demonstrate the superority of the Christian faith to Judaism. He has this in mind when he writes:

> The law was given through Moses; grace and truth came through Jesus Christ. (1:17)

Moses did not give the Jews "bread from heaven"; Jesus is true bread from heaven and he has come because the Father has sent him (6:32). Worship is no longer to be centered in Jerusalem (4:21). A new temple for worship is now here (2:19–21). "The Jews" reject Jesus. He came to his own people and they did not accept him (1:11).

At the time of writing, the church and the synagogue were in opposition to each other and the polemics that character- ized that opposition appear to be reflected in the hostile dialogues recorded in John, chs. 6 to 9. We can understand the historical factors that led to the manner in which John speaks of "the Jews." At the same time, this does not give us a license to speak the same way and to refer to Jews in general as "children of the devil" as John has done (8:44). This is the language of controversy and heated debate. Surely, it cannot be considered a normative viewpoint for Christians toward Jews. John with its stress on the universal love of God should never be used to support or foster anti-Semitism or any other prejudicial attitude toward people whether they respond to the Christian message or do not do so. For John, the opposition of "the world" found special expression in the decree to excommunicate from the syna- gogue those who believed in Jesus. It was from this painful experience of rejection by official Judaism that the terminol- ogy of John regarding "the Jews" emerged. We can under- stand it, but we must not perpetuate it.

Christ's victory. John's dualism is a modified dualism. Christ has overcome the world (16:33) and the devil's complete defeat is predicted:

> Now is the judgment of this world, now shall the ruler of this
> world be cast out; and I, when I am lifted up from the earth,
> will draw all men to myself. (12:31–32)

The devil's defeat was for John more than a future event; it was in some sense a past triumph in which John rejoiced. Jesus had conquered by the glory of the cross and the resurrection. Jesus lay down his life and he took it again. By this he demonstrated his lordship. No one took it from him. Jesus accomplished the work that the Father sent him to perform here on earth. This is why when he says from the cross, "It is finished," he means more than the fact that his ministry has come to an end. Rather, he is proclaiming the fact that he has fully and completely accomplished his mission in the world. *"Consummatum est,"* were words of triumph and victory. The Christ was not defeated by "the ruler of this world," and the darkness of the world was unable to put out the light. The Word which had become flesh was now demonstrated to be CHRISTUS VICTOR, "Christ the Victorious One."

Dualism in Qumran. In both Qumran and John there is present a modified dualism. These two literatures are closer to each other in terminology at this point than either one is to the Old Testament.[6] We shall examine briefly the dualism found in the scrolls.

The literature at Qumran divides mankind into two groups: the sons of light and the sons of darkness. These two groups are ruled by two spirits, namely, "the spirits of truth and perversion." [7] The contrast between these two spirits is brought out in the following paragraph:

> From a spring of light (issue) the generations of truth; but
> from a fountain of darkness (issue) the generations of
> perverseness. In the hand of the prince of lights is the rule
> over all the sons of righteousness; in the ways of light they

walk. But in the hand of the angel of darkness is all the rule over the sons of perversion; and in the ways of darkness they walk.[8]

The power of darkness fights against the sons of righteousness.[9] The God of Israel and his "angel of truth" help the sons of light.[10] The dualism of the scrolls is not eternal but modified, for God "created the spirits of light and darkness," and the power of evil is limited in duration, for

God has . . . appointed a period for the existence of wrongdoing.[11]

The dualism began at a certain time and will end at a time appointed by God.

The Manual of Discipline explains that the work of the Spirit of Truth is

To enlighten the heart of man, and to make straight before him all the ways of righteousness.[12]

In contrast to this we read:

But to the spirit of perversion belongs greediness, indolence of the hands in the service of righteousness, wickedness and falsehood, pride and haughtiness of heart, . . . stiffness of neck and hardening the heart to walk in all the ways of darkness and crafty thought.[13]

The Manual says that God has set these two spirits "in equal parts until the last period." [14] There is eternal enmity between these two. They do not "walk together" but are characterized by "passionate strife" between them. In words of encouragement to the faithful remnant the Manual says concerning wrongdoing,

At the season of visitation He will destroy it forever; and then the truth of the world will appear forever.[15]

According to the scrolls the children of righteousness who are led by the Spirit of Truth are the men of the community who are living according to the law of Moses as it has been interpreted by the community.[16] Ultimate triumph for the community and for Truth are envisioned in The War of the Sons of Light and the Sons of Darkness. This scroll affirms that the people of God are destined to "come to dominion," whereas those who have cast their lot with Belial "shall be doomed to eternal extinction." It adds,

> And iniquity shall be vanquished, leaving no remnant; [for the sons] of darkness there shall be no escape.[17]

The dualism of Qumran is also expressed by the words "flesh" (*basar*, in Hebrew) and "Spirit." As in the case of the Greek word *sarx,* this word is used in both a neutral and an ethical sense. An example of the neutral use, in which "flesh" merely speaks of physical existence with the added connotation of frailty and limitation, is:

> But what is flesh (to be worthy) of this? What is a creature of clay for such great marvel to be done . . . ?[18]

There are other passages, however, where the word has a definite ethical and moral connotation. An example would be:

> And I, if I totter, God's dependable mercy is my salvation forever; and if I stumble in the guilt of flesh, my justification through God's righteousness will stand everlastingly.[19]

Summarizing the concept of dualism in the literature of Qumran, we can make the following observations:

1. The dualism is a religious and ethical dualism, not a physical one. Matter is not per se viewed as evil. The ethical dualism is closely linked to obedience to the law of Moses as interpreted by the Qumran sectarians.

2. The dualism is not an eternal one. The spirits of light and darkness are created spirits. God is above both of them. The dualism had a beginning and will also have an end.

3. The dualism will end in the triumph of good over evil, of the spirit of light over the spirit of darkness, and of the sons of light over the sons of darkness.

4. The dualism is more than an external dualism, it is an internal one. In the heart of each man the two spirits are present. A man is a son of light if he heeds the spirit of light, but he is a child of darkness if he yields to the spirit of darkness.

5. God will reward the sons of light, but only ruin awaits the sons of darkness.

The origin of dualism in the literature of Qumran. It is well known that dualism was a prominent feature of Iranian thought in the centuries immediately before Christ. In the scriptures of Zoroastrianism there is an emphasis upon two spirits, one good and the other evil. It is characteristic of Iranian dualism to speak of the two opposing forces in terms of light and darkness. The similarities between Qumran and Iranian dualism led K. G. Kuhn to conclude that the scrolls at this point reflect Iranian influence.[20] There appears to be one great difference between them: in Zoroastrianism the good spirits and the evil spirits are coexistent, independent, uncreated forces; in Qumran thought they are both created by God. As Raymond E. Brown has pointed out:

> The imported dualism of Qumran has come into contact with the Old Testament theology of God the Creator, and is subservient to that great truth.[21]

Even the dualism in Iranian thought is to some extent a modified dualism in the sense that it is limited in time. The ultimate triumph of Ahura Mazda (the Spirit of Light) and of good is definitely predicted. The influence of Iranian thought on theological expressions at Qumran is understandable in view of the contact the Jews had with Iran during the time of the exile and in the centuries thereafter. What distinguished the Qumran literature at this point from the Old Testament is simply the greater degree of absorption of ideas into their literature. The Old Testament appears not to have remained isolated from the light-darkness dualism motif of Zoroastrianism, but it is not present to the same degree that it is found at Qumran.

Comparison of dualism in Qumran and the Fourth Gospel. Comparing the concepts of dualism as found in Qumran and in the Fourth Gospel, we note the following similarities and differences:

1. Both stress a religious dualism that is not basically physical.

2. The dualism in both cases is neither absolute nor final. Both are a modified dualism.

3. Both express the dualism in terminology which in a number of instances is highly similar. Especially noted were such terms as light and darkness, flesh and spirit, and the expression "Spirit of Truth." The Fourth Gospel has a richer variety of expressions to speak of this dualism, as, for example, the antitheses: life and death, from above and from below, bondage and freedom, sight and blindness, this world and "not of this world."

In terms of differences, the following characteristics should be mentioned:

1. In the scrolls the two spirits are said to be present in every man. In the Fourth Gospel the dualism is more external than internal. As Colwell and Titus have written:

> The Johannine believer is not a dualistic microcosm, a being in which the struggle of good and evil worlds is carried on in miniature. The struggle between good and evil, light and darkness, upper and lower takes place outside the believer; it is an external process in which Jesus triumphed.[22]

The believer shares in the triumph through believing in Jesus.

A person is either from above or from below. Either he has the Spirit of Truth or he does not. A person is loyal to one of the two realms which are in conflict. This stands in contrast to the Dead Sea Scrolls which envision two spirits in every man, the spirit of good and the spirit of evil. The particular emphasis that is found in the Fourth Gospel probably owes much to the particular situation in which the author and his readers were placed. They were a struggling minority in a generally hostile religious and social environment. To belong to this little company demanded courage and decision. This was no time for divided loyalties. Hence the sharp division between those who were "of the world" and those who had been "chosen out of the world."

2. The dualism in the scrolls is climaxed according to the War Scroll in a physical conflict between the sons of light and the sons of darkness. While a conflict bearing certain similarities to this is envisoned in the book of Revelation, no such battle is mentioned in the Fourth Gospel. The Fourth Gospel is not apocalyptic, and although it speaks of the future, it does so primarily in terms of the consummation of salvation for the individual believer who will be with Christ in the Father's presence. On the whole, however, John's eschatological stress is on the present reality of God's blessings, that is, on "realized eschatology." In contrast to physical conflict Jesus says in John:

> My kingship is not of this world; if my kingship were of this world, my servants would fight, that I might not be handed over to the Jews; but my kingship is not from the world. (18:36)

Whereas the scrolls focus on a cosmic warfare between two spirits, John stresses the contrast between two worlds, the one "above" and the other "below." [23] Charlesworth argues that in John, Jesus struggles against the world and not an evil spirit.[24] James L. Price, on the other hand, draws attention to the references in John to "the devil," "Satan," and "the ruler of this world" (12:31; 13:2, 27; 14:30; 16:11). He then adds,

> The tantalizingly brief references to this cosmic dimension of Johannine dualism probably bring the theology of the Fourth Gospel closer to Qumran dualism than many scholars have allowed.[25]

It seems best not to draw too sharp a contrast here between Qumran and John. The cosmic aspect of Johannine dualism is expressed more clearly and forcefully in the First Letter.[26] Since John stressed the realized aspects of Christian eschatology, the emphasis is not on a future cosmic conflict but on Christ's present "cosmic victory." [27]

3. The dualism in the scrolls puts a great emphasis on keeping the law of Moses and also on observing the distinctive regulations of the sect. It stresses asceticism and ethics. The sons of light are those who live according to the strict regulations of the Qumran community. In the case of the Fourth Gospel it is not a question of adherence to any set code of ethics or of conduct that distinguishes the sons of light from the sons of darkness. It is a question of belief in Jesus as the Christ. This call for commitment to him stands in sharp contrast to the esoteric, ascetic, and legalistic doctrines of Qumran.

Comparison of dualism in Gnosticism and the Fourth Gospel. It has been noted that the dualism of John and that of Qumran were not physical. They did not sharply distinguish and separate matter and spirit. Gnosticism, on the other hand, does this. While John uses certain Gnostic terminology, he does not share this Gnostic doctrine. Flesh and matter in Gnosticism are evil. If John had shared that view, he could never have penned 1:14. J. N. Sanders has written:

> That the Christ has come in the flesh was the great stumbling-block to the Gnostics. John boldly used the language of his

contemporaries in order to help them to understand a faith radically different from their own, however similar it may sound superficially.[28]

Sanders expressed the same thought elsewhere in these words:

> John's theology tends to deal in contrasts. . . . But though it sounds dualistic, it has nothing more than its language in common with the ontological dualism characteristic of Gnosticism.[29]

It appears that the author of the Fourth Gospel was reacting against certain ideas found in early Gnosticism and yet at the same time he reflects much of the vocabulary popular in Gnostic writings. He does not share the ascetic note of Gnosticism nor the belief of the Gnostics in the wickedness of matter. Salvation is not escape from the evil world of matter. As Colwell and Titus have written,

> He substitutes the antithesis of Christian versus non-Christian for the Gnostic antithesis of matter and spirit.[30]

It seems clear that when the dualisms of John, Qumran, and Gnosticism are compared, John bears a much closer resemblance to the thought of Qumran than to that of Gnosticism. In fact, John appears to be opposing certain ideas which Gnosticism stressed, such as the fact that matter is evil, that God could therefore not have created the world, for he is good, and that Jesus could not have had a real physical body. The anti-Gnostic elements which begin to emerge in the Gospel of John are much more forcefully argued in I John.

Where did John's dualism originate? In view of the similarities between John and Qumran should we conclude that the Fourth Gospel derived its outlook and vocabulary from this sect? This conclusion appears not to be warranted. Dualism is a concept which to some degree "colors almost every form of religious thinking in the Greco-Roman world." [31] Nor are the terminology of the Fourth Gospel and that of Qumran so uniquely similar as to be isolated and distinctive examples of this type of dualistic terminology. A few examples from a variety of sources will show that this is the case.

Dualism in other literature of the period. In a number of books of the Pseudepigrapha similarities to the dualism found in the scrolls have been noted. An example would be:

> Know, therefore, my children, that two spirits wait upon man—the spirit of truth and the spirit of deceit.[32]

As in the case of the scrolls, the Testament of the Twelve Patriarchs (which was known and used at Qumran) sees the conflict between the spirits as going on within man. It is an internal struggle:

> Two ways hath God given to the sons of men and two inclinations, and two kinds of action, and two modes (of action), and two issues. . . . For there are two ways of good and evil, and with these are the two inclinations in our breasts discriminating them.[33]

This document, like the scrolls, predicts that the power of evil will, in God's time, be put down and light and darkness will then be supreme.

Turning to the apostle Paul, one finds in his writings a very pronounced dualism. It is of a religious nature and employs to some extent the light-darkness terminology which is in the scrolls and also in the Fourth Gospel. The expression "sons of light" is also used by Paul. Examples of Pauline dualism are:

> But you are not in darkness, brethren, for that day to surprise you like a thief. For you are all sons of light and sons of the day; we are not of the night or of darkness. (I Thess. 5:4–5)

Do not be mismated with unbelievers. For what partnership have righteousness and iniquity? Or what fellowship has light with darkness? What accord has Christ with Belial? Or what has a believer in common with an unbeliever? (II Cor. 6:14–15)

It will be noted that in the above statements Paul places on one side the expressions "sons of light," "sons of the day," "righteousness," "light," "believer," and "Christ." On the other side, and in contrast to the above expressions, he places "darkness," "iniquity," "unbelievers," and "Belial." The terminology closely resembles that of the scrolls, with the exception of the contrast between Christ and Belial. (Fre quent references to Belial do occur in the scrolls.) Also the expression "believer" would mean for Paul a believer in Christ rather than a faithful adherent to the regulations of the sect of Qumran. The similarity in terminology, with the above-mentioned exceptions, points out clearly that the language of the Qumran writers is not something exclusive or unique. Others shared their religious vocabulary to a great extent. The exact connotations given to words differed, of course, with the group using them.

In the Synoptics there are a few expressions of a dualism which resembles that found in the scrolls and in the Fourth Gospel but it is not nearly as common as it is in Qumran and in John. Examples of the equation of "light" with the truth would be:

You are the light of the world. . . . Let your light so shine before men that they may see your good works and give glory to your Father who is in heaven. (Matt. 5:14, 16)

The master commended the dishonest steward for his prudence; for the sons of this world are wiser in their generation than the sons of light. (Luke 16:8)

The last example has the contrast between "the sons of this world" and "the sons of light." This is quite similar to the dualism of the scrolls.

Terminology that resembles the phrasing of the dualism found in the scrolls and in the Fourth Gospel is also found in such early Christian literature as the Didache, the Epistle of Barnabas, and the Shepherd of Hermas. In the Epistle of Barnabas we read:

> There are two ways of teaching and authority: that of light and that of darkness. And there is a great difference between the two ways. For over the one are appointed light-bearing angels of God, but over the other, angels of Satan.[34]

In the Shepherd of Hermas there is a section which speaks of two angels being present with every man. This resembles the doctrine of the scrolls which says that each man has "two spirits"—the spirit of truth and the spirit of perversity. The passage in question reads as follows:

> "Now hear," he said, "about faith. There are two angels with man, one of uprightness and one of evil. . . . The angel of righteousness is delicate and modest and meek and quiet. . . . Now observe the works of the evil angel. First of all, he is ill tempered and bitter and foolish, and his works are evil, destroying the servants of God." [35]

The angel of uprightness is said to come into the mind and to seek to guide man into good actions. The angel of wickedness comes and seeks to tempt man into wicked actions. Thus there appears to be a personification of the temptations which are present in the heart of man. It is clear that the mode of thought reflected in the Shepherd of Hermas bears a close resemblance to the teaching of the scrolls on the two spirits, the one of truth and the other of perversity.

Summary and conclusions. The dualism found in Qumran and in the Fourth Gospel is expressed in much the same terminology in various contemporary literatures. This immediately raises the question whether it is correct to draw the conclusion that the scrolls directly influenced the Fourth

Gospel. It is more probable that both literatures reflect something of a common background. Both writings might be considered as providing us with separate windows opening up to our view a small part of the religious landscape of the ancient world during the years immediately before and after Christ.

It appears that what we have in Qumran and in the Fourth Gospel are two examples of a theological terminology that had become diffused in the Middle East at that time. Both literatures share in the theological thought world of their day. This theological atmosphere had within it strains from many sources, including Hebraic, Iranian, and Greek elements. Palestine was not an island set in isolation. It was a cultural crossroads. This has been well expressed by W. D. Davies:

> The first century milieu . . . was variegated and, above all, complex. In particular has it become clear that the traditional convenient dichotomy between Judaism and Hellenism was largely false. In the fusions of the first century the boundaries between these are now seen to have been very fluid.[36]

What Davies says of Judaism and Hellenism can to some extent apply to Iranian thought as well. Iranian ideas did not by some invisible barrier restrain their influence to a small geographical area around the Dead Sea. The Jews had a common religious and historical background. Iranian thought appears to have influenced Judaism in a number of areas—for example, the belief in the resurrection, and also the sharpening of the division between the two spiritual forces in the world, light and darkness, God and Satan.

It would appear then that the dualism of the Qumran community is not directly responsible for the dualism of the Fourth Gospel. Both literatures, to the degree in which they have similarity in thought and expressions with respect to their dualism, reflect a strain of the religious thought of their time and they would appear to do so independently.

Meaning for today. John's dualism is determined by his Christology. How we respond to Jesus determines for the author whether we are "children of God" or not. There is implied here a strong call for decision. He seeks commitment and the kind of commitment that is willing to suffer persecution, if need be, for the name and message of Jesus. The impact of the early church was great, for it stood in such sharp contrast to surrounding culture. Today in America we have developed a kind of civil religion in which the interests of church and state seem to have coalesced in large measure into a generally conservative stance that seeks to preserve inherited patterns of thought and action without much critical examination of these in the light of Scriptural standards and imperatives. John's Gospel with its Christocentric, and ultimately theocentric, perspective can provide us with a proper base from which to reexamine past patterns of behavior and our present system of values. While a system that sees everything as either white or black, light or darkness, may be too simplistic, it nevertheless can stand as a corrective for the tendency of many not to have strong convictions about religious and moral values. The church cannot ultimately become the servant of the state nor captive to the cultural values of its secular environment if it is to retain a proper sense of its identity and if it is to be an effective agent for creative and helpful change and renewal in our generation. John's message reminds the church and individual believers as well of their unique identity and of their distinctive responsibilities in the world.

10

~~~~~~

Truth

The words "truth" *(alētheia)* and "true" *(alēthēs, alēthinos)* stand out in the Gospel of John as favorite and significant words which occur with a much higher frequency than they do in the Synoptic Gospels. The following list illustrates the degree to which these words are characteristic of the vocabulary of Johannine literature.

	Matt.	Mark	Luke	John	I,II,III John	Rev.
alētheia ("truth")	1	3	3	25	20	0
alēthēs ("true")	1	1	0	14	3	0
alēthinos ("true")	0	0	1	9	4	10
Totals	2	4	4	48	27	10

What is distinctive about John is not only the fact that these words occur much more often but also that they are given new meaning and significance as compared to their usage in the Synoptics.

The Meanings of Truth

The meaning of "truth" and "true" in the Synoptic Gospels. The word "truth" *(alētheia)* occurs in the Synoptics seven times and it always carries the connotation of veracity or dependability. In six instances the proper translation is "truthfully," "in truth," or "certainly." In the seventh occurrence it means to tell "the whole truth." None of these seven uses carries any religious connotation, as "truth" characteristically does in John.

The word "true" *(alēthēs)* is found in Matt. 22:16 and in the parallel verse in Mark 12:14. The verse reads, "Master, we know that you are true." Both then add the phrase, "and teach the way of God truthfully." The second phrase helps to interpret the meaning of the earlier statement. Jesus is "true" because he is an honest and reliable teacher.

The adjective "true" *(alēthinos)* occurs only once in the Synoptics. Luke quotes the words of Jesus:

> If then you have not been faithful in the unrighteous mammon, who will entrust to you *the true riches?* (Luke 16:11)

"True" riches are those which are permanent and never disappear or disappoint.

In all these occurrences veracity, dependability, reliability, or honesty are the key ideas. None of these usages carries the distinctive connotations that John attaches to the words "true" and "truth."

The meaning of "truth" and "true" in John. One of the most central of all statements in John is the affirmation that Jesus is the giver, source, and very being of truth (1:14,17; 14:6).

Jesus bears witness to the truth (5:33; 18:37) and "speaks" the truth (8:40,45,46; 16:7). The disciples have come to know the truth (8:32; 16:13) and the truth has set them free (8:32). The devil has nothing to do with the truth because the truth is not in him (8:44). Concerning the disciples, however, Jesus prays that they may be consecrated in the truth (17:17,19). The Holy Spirit is uniquely spoken of as "the Spirit of Truth" (14:17; 15:26; 16:13). God's word is truth (17:17). Worship "in spirit and truth" is the worship that God desires (4:23–24). He who "does the truth" comes to the light (3:21; cf. I John 1:6).

John's penchant for the dramatic phrase and situation is illustrated in the scene in which Jesus stands before Pilate and Pilate asks the question, "What is truth?" (18:38). The writer and the readers of the Gospel of John know that Truth at that moment stands before Pilate, but the political ruler fails to recognize or acknowledge him. By implication Truth confronts each reader of the Fourth Gospel. Those who are "of the truth" will confess Jesus as the Christ, the Son of God. Those who are not "of the truth" will, like Pilate, turn away in unbelief.

It is clear from the various passages cited that the concept of "truth" has become in John a central and dominant religious motif which he associates specifically with Jesus as the revealer of the Father. Those who respond to Jesus by believing in him receive "the Spirit of Truth" and "do the truth." They have been set free by the truth, they worship the Father in "spirit and truth," and they are consecrated "in the truth." This means that not only Jesus but believers bear a special relationship to "truth." Since this very elaborate development of ideas around "truth" is not paralleled in the Synoptic Gospels, the question may properly be asked from what source John has derived his distinctive vocabulary and emphasis. Conflicting answers have been proposed. Does he use "truth" with its classical Greek connotation, or is his thought more closely tied to Hebraic ideas? Or is it a combination of these with certain unique emphases that are distinctively his?

"Truth" in Greek thought. In Greek thought, *alētheia* means "truth" and is viewed as the opposite of "lie" or "mere appearance." It implies "reality." When used of persons it means "truthfulness" and "sincerity." [1] It is "fundamentally an intellectual category." [2]

"Truth" in Hebrew thought. The word for "Truth" in Hebrew is *'emet*. It carries the connotations of "firmness," "faithfulness," and "reliability." [3] It is not only an intellectual category but a moral one.[4]

Some authors see John's usage to be predominantly patterned after Greek thought.[5] E. F. Scott[6] sought to trace John's usage back to Plato's doctrine of ideas. He believed that at this point John took over and modified Plato's concept of truth as he found it expressed in Philo.

C. H. Dodd and W. F. Howard both acknowledge that in John's Gospel occur expressions that reflect Hebrew influence. C. H. Dodd recognizes that the expression "to do the truth" (3:21) would be one that a Greek reader would feel to be "definitely strange to the natural idiom of the language." [7] He interprets the phrase to mean "to practice fidelity" and cites as Old Testament examples of this usage Gen. 32:10; 47:29. Despite the fact that a few other passages appear at first glance also to echo Old Testament expressions, Dodd[8] concludes that John's use is predominantly influenced by common Greek usage and that it means primarily that which is "real." He points out, however, that knowing the truth in John involves union with Jesus, who is the truth. Therefore even though truth is intellectualized in John, it goes beyond mere intellectual apprehension. W. F. Howard[9] points out other passages that reflect Old Testament influence. He cites

John 1:14 and the phrase "full of grace and truth" which is based on the Hebrew phrase which is rendered "steadfast love and faithfulness" (Ex. 34:6). Howard recognizes the Jewish coloring of the Johannine language but he still argues that the word "truth" has its Greek meaning of "reality." [10] These interpreters were correct in recognizing Hebraic elements but they were still too much inclined to treat John as basically Greek in its main thrust.

A shift of emphasis in recent years. In the Dead Sea Scrolls two distinct Johannine expressions have appeared. These are "to do the truth" (1QS 1.5; 5:3) and the expression "spirit of truth." These interesting parallels have led to a reconsideration of the degree to which John reflects Greek thought. Does he mean by truth "reality," as maintained by the earlier authors cited?

Yrjö Alanen[11] maintains that while for Greek thought knowledge of truth has an objective character and that it is only through an intellectual process that a man can acquire it, in Hebrew thought truth is personal and its appropriation relates to heart and conscience. The hindrance to the acquiring of truth is not a weak intellect but a hardened heart and prideful trust in one's own reason. The appropriation of truth, according to the Bible, is dependent upon the right disposition of the heart, a sincere character, and a willingness to listen. All of this leads Alanen to understand *alētheia* in the New Testament in terms of the Hebrew *'emet.* In both the Old and the New Testament, he argues, truth in its highest meaning is understood as the revealed word of God. In the New Testament we encounter Jesus as the personal Truth (14:6). It is therefore in the context of Hebrew and not Greek thought that John's teaching on truth is to be interpreted. Alanen's conclusions appear to be valid.

I. de la Potterie has argued that both the literature of Qumran and the use of "truth" in John reflect the influence of

Jewish apocalyptic writings and the Wisdom tradition. Here we encounter repeatedly such phrases as "walking in the truth" and "doing the truth." In the Wisdom literature the expression "truth" is synonymous with "wisdom." This leads de la Potterie[12] to conclude that truth is not the metaphysical reality of God in the Hellenistic sense but the truth of God revealed in the incarnate Christ. De la Potterie argues persuasively that the literary tradition to which the author of the Fourth Gospel belongs is not that of Hellenism or of dualistic Gnosticism but of postexilic Judaism. John has taken up several expressions used previously and when he creates new ones he remains in the same line of thought development.

INTERPRETING JOHN'S DISTINCTIVE USAGE

John's unique contribution. The tendency to focus more on Hebrew versus Greek thought does not mean that John's thought can be fully explained by tracing it to apocalyptic and Wisdom literature. He is a creative writer who has made his own unique contribution. Truth for John is centered in Jesus, who has come to bring men salvation. Josef Blank[13] put it well when he wrote that truth in John must be understood Christologically. This is the key to John's meaning of truth. Above everything else, "truth" in John is the "revelation and salvation truth" which has been granted us in Jesus Christ.[14] Or, as Alf Corell[15] has expressed it, truth in John embraces the totality of Christian redemption in Christ.

1. *Jesus is "the truth."* When John affirms this about Jesus he does not mean that Jesus is "reality" in the Greek sense of that which is real in contrast to that which is unreal or only appearance. Nor does the expression stress Jesus' faithfulness in keeping with the Hebrew meaning of the word *'emet.* John here stresses that Jesus is the only complete and total revelation of the Father. It is simply another way of

proclaiming that he who has seen Jesus has seen the Father. This does not equate Jesus with the Father but affirms that the Father has made himself known through Jesus Christ and that it is only in Jesus and not in Moses or in any other person that this full revelation has been given.[16]

2. *"Truth" in John and the Hebrew connotation of "faithfulness."* The Hebrew theme of "faithfulness" is not neglected by John. It appears to be expressed in at least two special uses in the Fourth Gospel. The first of these occurs in 1:14, where it is said of the incarnate Word that he was "full of grace and truth." This expression seems to be based on the familiar double formula of the Old Testament, *chesed we'emet*, namely, "steadfast love and faithfulness" (Ps. 25:10), attributes of the God of Israel. Since the Word is declared by John to be God, it is not inappropriate that these qualities should be transferred in the Fourth Gospel from God to the Word, for it is through the Word that God has manifested himself among men.

Another use in John which appears to carry the connotation of faithfulness is when Jesus speaks of himself as "the true vine." Sometimes this adjective can be interpreted as meaning "real" versus that which is only claimed to be valid. For example, Jesus is the "real light," not John the Baptist, as some seem to have believed (1:9).[17] In a passage such as 15:1, however, where Jesus is the "true vine," he is clearly being contrasted with Israel which in the Old Testament is declared to be God's vine (Ps. 80:8–17; Isa. 5:1–7; Jer. 2:21; 12:10; Ezek. 15:2–8; 19:10–14). Where Israel was unfaithful in its responsibilities to Yahweh, Jesus was faithful and obedient to his heavenly Father. Hence Jesus and not Israel (which in the Old Testament is called God's son, Hos. 11:1) is the true vine.

It would seem that the adjective "good" in the phrase "I am the good shepherd" (10:11) is being used in the Fourth Gospel as basically synonymous with "true." The contrast is with the faithless shepherds of Israel (Jer. 2:8; 10:21; 12:10;

23:1–5; Ezek. 34:1–24) who feed themselves, look after their own welfare and safety, and neglect and mistreat the flock. In calling Jesus the "good" shepherd, the author of the Fourth Gospel presents Jesus as the shepherd who does not pursue his own interests but loves the sheep and lays down his life on their behalf. Bultmann[18] suggests that while John could have used the adjective "true" here instead of "good," his choice of the latter is simply due to the fact that it is a customary and appropriate descriptive adjective for shepherds.

3. *"Worship in spirit and truth" (4:24)*. To worship "in spirit and truth" means more than to be genuine in worship. The Gospel of John is not attacking insincere worship. We cannot here neglect the basic Johannine identification of truth first with Jesus and secondly with the revelation which he brings through his person, actions, and words. "Truth" in John is always Christocentric. Therefore to worship in spirit and truth means to worship in accordance with the new revelation of God which has come to humanity in and through Jesus Christ. It means first and foremost a willingness to join with Thomas in his model confession, "My Lord and my God!" The use of "spirit" here in conjunction with "truth" inevitably reminds us of John's expression "the Spirit of truth." True worshipers will have the Spirit, for the Father and the Son have sent the Spirit to be with them (14:16). Worship in the spirit in John in all probability implies worship through the Holy Spirit.[19] Only those who confess that Jesus is the Christ have the Spirit, according to John, for it is Jesus who gives the Spirit to those who believe on him (7:39; 14:16,17; 20:22).

Some have suggested that by the above expression John also implies right conduct both in attitude and action.[20] Since ethics plays such a minor role in John, one wonders whether parallels in the scrolls can properly be used to interpret John's meaning at this point. It may be reading more into John than he intended.

4. *"Doing the truth" (3:21).* This phrase occurs in the Qumran literature[21] and also in the Old Testament.[22] Hebrew rather than Greek usage is evident here. Greek does not speak of "doing the truth." Truth for the Greeks was something taught or learned, not done. In the Old Testament this expression implies behavior that is trustworthy and faithful. In John, "doing the truth" is tied to "coming to the light" (3:21). This refers to believing in Jesus, which for John is "the work of God" (6:29), that is, the work that God demands. In I John there seems to be an expansion of this idea, for to faith there is added proper behavior:

> If we say we have fellowship with him while we walk in darkness, we lie and do not live according to the truth [literally, "we are not doing the truth"]. (I John 1:6)

In II and III John we find the phrase "following the truth" (II John 4; III John 3–4). Here orthodox doctrine seems to be the predominant idea. There appears to be here less of the vibrant, creative motif which we see attached to "truth" in the Gospel of John in which the person of Jesus is the focal point. Instead, we seem to have a rather stock phrase which stresses orthodox theology in the face of the threat of heresy.

5. *"The Spirit of truth" (14:17; 15:26; 16:13).* In the use of the description "the Spirit of truth," John shows a close affinity to the scrolls of Qumran, where this phrase also occurs (1QS 3:13–4:26). There the expression *ruach 'emet* ("spirit of truth") stands in contrast to "spirit of deceit." In every man these two spirits strive for mastery. At Qumran "the spirit of truth" is viewed as an angel and the struggle is cosmic as well as an internal one. In John the Spirit of truth is identified with the Holy Spirit, also called the Paraclete. He comes to continue the work of Jesus.

The use of the same expressions in Qumran and John is quite interesting. In all probability they reflect an indebtedness to some earlier use of the term in the intertestamental period.[23] There is sufficient divergence in meaning between John and Qumran that a direct dependence of John on Qumran appears unlikely. A common source is probable. Each community seems to have adapted and modified the expression in accordance with its distinctive theologies.

It may be that the expression "the Spirit of truth" is a key to John's whole treatment of truth. Jesus gives the Spirit. If this Spirit is viewed as "the Spirit of truth," then Jesus is automatically related to the "truth," for the Spirit bears witness to him. It may also be that the close tie between truth and wisdom in the Wisdom literature contributed to the development of John's teaching concerning truth, since John uses wisdom motifs in developing his Christology.[24]

Summary and conclusions. What is distinctive about John's use of "truth" is the fact that it is Christocentric. Jesus is the truth about the Father. He is the one in and through whom the Father is revealed. By responding to Jesus, that is, by believing in him as the Christ, the truth becomes ours. For John the opposite of truth is more than error. It is blindness, bondage, and death. Truth is therefore tied directly to John's understanding of salvation.

John's approach is dogmatic. It is deliberately so. John rejects all other claimants to truth with an absoluteness that leads him to say of the Jews who reject Jesus that they are children of the devil (8:44). This accusation strikes us as very harsh, even when we acknowledge that it is addressed not to the Jewish people at large but to the religious hierarchy. While we too would wish to affirm that the ultimate revelation of the Father has come in Jesus Christ, we would probably wish to acknowledge that God has not left himself without a witness in Judaism and in other world religions.

We would wish to affirm what is worthy in these faiths rather than to condemn them categorically. There is today an increased appreciation of the great debt which the Christian faith owes to Judaism. The situation of conflict out of which the Gospel of John emerged led to a minimizing of this indebtedness. But even here we find that Jesus says to the woman at the well, "Salvation is from the Jews" (4:22). John is, therefore, not totally unappreciative of the heritage of Judaism. This we too will wish to acknowledge. Perhaps we would give it a greater prominence than John has done. At the same time we would stand with John and bear witness to our faith by confessing that we have found in Jesus Christ "the way, and the truth, and the life" (14:6).

11

The Spirit
of Truth

John puts much less stress on the Spirit working through Jesus in his ministry than do the Synoptics. There is no mention of a miraculous birth by the Spirit, of being thrust into the wilderness by the Spirit, of returning in the power of the Spirit to begin his ministry, or of casting out demons and performing miracles by the Spirit. These are stressed in the Synoptics but not in John. John does mention that the Spirit descends on Jesus and remains with him (1:32–33), so that the distinction between John and the Synoptics should not be overstressed. F. Mussner[1] warns against making the distinction between John and the Synoptics too great. Nevertheless it is true that John's perspective is primarily futuristic. Jesus will give the Spirit, but this will not take place until after his death and resurrection (7:39). The stress is not on the Spirit directing Jesus' earthly ministry but on the function of the Spirit as continuing and completing the ministry of Jesus after his departure.[2]

In the New Testament, only the Gospel of John calls the Holy Spirit by the titles "the Spirit of truth" and "the Paraclete." There are in John five major promises of the

164

giving of the Spirit found in the farewell discourses. In these predictions the Spirit is described in a fivefold manner. He is viewed and presented as:

1. An abiding Presence (14:16–17)
2. A Teacher (14:25–26)
3. A Witness (15:26)
4. A Convictor (16:7–11)
5. A Guide (16:13–15)

Because of this concentration in John on teaching concerning the Spirit, it has not inappropriately been referred to as "The Gospel of the Spirit." [3]

The Spirit as the Paraclete. In four places John refers to the Spirit as the *parakletos.* The only other place in the Bible where this word is used is in I John 2:1, where Jesus in his present ministry in the presence of God is spoken of as the *parakletos* of the believers. There he pleads our case before the Father. He is viewed as a defense attorney. He speaks on our behalf. He is presented as an advocate who is "the righteous one." The basis of Jesus' intercession on our behalf is the fact that by his own death, atonement has been made. I John speaks of Jesus as "the expiation (propitiation) for our sins, and not for ours only but also for the sins of the whole world" (I John 2:2).

In John's presentation of the Spirit as the Paraclete there is also a forensic connotation. He speaks on Jesus' behalf and bears witness to him (15:26). He declares the fact that Jesus was "the righteous one" and that therefore he was unjustly put to death (16:8–10). In these roles the Spirit acts in a manner that can be compared to that of a defense lawyer. At the same time his work includes that of convicting the world of sin. Here his role is more like that of a prosecuting attorney (16:8–9). Hence there is the note of judgment (16:8,11).

In addition to the forensic connotations the Paraclete is

viewed as an abiding presence (of Jesus and of the Father), a teacher, and a guide. Since the word *paraklētos* has more than one connotation, various translations have been suggested for it. In the King James Version it is rendered "Comforter." This translation does not originate with the 1611 version but is dependent on the rendering given in the fourteenth century in John Wycliffe's translation. Originally the word "Comforter" appears to have retained some of the meaning of the Latin root upon which the word is built. The Latin behind "Comforter" is the word *fortis,* meaning "brave," "strong," "courageous." This meaning is quite different from our modern understanding of the word "comforter." Today we think of such ideas as consoling or sympathizing with someone when we speak of comforting. Obviously John did not have this as his primary meaning. It certainly does not express the ideas of teaching, guiding, and convicting. Nor does it capture the important idea of the Spirit coming to strengthen the disciples so that they may be brave and strong witnesses of Jesus after his departure from them. The translations "Strengthener" and "Helper" would in modern English be preferable to "Comforter."

The translation in the Revised Standard Version, "Counselor," seems to be no improvement. Perhaps the translators had in mind a lawyer, who is sometimes referred to as "counselor," but it is more likely to suggest the image of a person to whom someone goes for counseling. Another possible way to express this word in English is simply to refer to the *paraklētos* as our "advocate." This is how it is rendered in Weymouth's translation and in the New English Bible. Literally *paraklētos* can mean "One called alongside to help." The Latin equivalent for this is *advocatus* (*ad* plus *vocare,* literally "to call to oneself"). This rendering has the merit of being a literal rendering of what the Greek says. At the same time it conjures up in our mind a modern image of the law court and of the legal profession. Such a meaning is too narrow for John's concept of the Spirit and therefore even the word "advocate" has clear limitations. Perhaps the best solution is to do what Jewish writers did. They transliterated the Greek word into Hebrew rather than attempt to translate it. They simply wrote *prqlyt* and let the context suggest the meaning.[4] Some have concluded that the safest way to proceed is to do the same in English as was done in Hebrew and to use the word "Paraclete."[5] This allows the context to determine the meaning rather than to have the reader import irrelevant connotations from the twentieth century into the text. Neither does it focus on one aspect of the Spirit's work to the neglect of others.

Origin of the concept of the Paraclete. No Hebrew word has as yet been found of which *paraklētos* is a direct translation. There is no exact equivalent in the Old Testament. Bultmann[6] suggested that this concept might have had its origin in proto-Mandaean ideas, but the tendency today is to look to possible Jewish antecedents instead.[7] As Raymond E. Brown[8] points out, no exact parallel has been found in any Jewish literature, including the Qumran Scrolls, but the basic functions of the Paraclete seem all to be expressed in one way or another in Jewish literature. Sometimes Wisdom offers a parallel and at other times an angelic being or spirit does what in John the Paraclete is said to do. Whatever influence may have come to John from these sources, it is clear that his treatment is unique, especially, in his distinctive affirmation that in the coming of the Paraclete, Jesus returns and that through the Paraclete he continues his work. John's treatment of the Paraclete theme is unique also in the New Testament. John uses this designation for the Spirit only in his role after Jesus' departure. It is in the distinct capacity of the one who continues Jesus' ministry that he speaks of the Spirit in this way. Consequently the designation "Paraclete" is more restricted than the expressions "the Spirit" or "the

Holy Spirit." These latter terms are more general and comprehensive than the expression "the Paraclete." Consequently certain functions are attributed to the Spirit which are not said of the Paraclete.[9] An illustration would be Jesus' statement to Nicodemus concerning being born of the Spirit (3:5). Clearly the Spirit and the Paraclete are one, but the title "Paraclete" focuses on a special function and capacity of the Spirit. The distinctions should not be stressed in such a way as to suggest that John does not equate the Holy Spirit and the Paraclete. A. R. C. Leaney, for example, argues that, for John, the Paraclete is primarily God himself.[10] He also maintains that the Spirit which is promised in 14:26 is not the Holy Spirit but a spirit in the sense of a personal being like the angels spoken of in the intertestamental literature. To do this he questions the accuracy of the present text of 14:26 which does equate the Paraclete with the Holy Spirit. There is, however, no textual variant at this point which would support the change that Leaney suggests. Since John is writing several decades into the Christian era, it is also highly questionable that the Qumran teaching about an angelic being ("the spirit of truth") can be transferred to John and made the basis for interpreting John's meaning. John's teaching reflects a theological perspective which has progressed far beyond the Qumran "spirit of truth."

The Spirit of Truth. In the Bible the expression "the Spirit of truth" is found only in John 14:17; 15:26; 16:13; and I John 4:6. The phrase is also found in the literature of Qumran. This is an important parallel, for it indicates that this expression which could quite easily be interpreted as being Greek in background (and before the Qumran discoveries was often so interpreted) is demonstrated to be quite at home in Jewish thinking. John and Qumran differ in the way they use these terms. In Qumran "the spirit of truth" stands in contrast to and in opposition to the "spirit of error." In

Qumran this struggle is both cosmic (with an eschatological climactic battle) and at the same time very personal, for the two spirits struggle in the heart of every man. In the Gospel of John the adversary is called the devil and Satan. He opposes Jesus and God rather than the spirit of truth. The identification of the role of the spirit of truth with the continuing presence and work of Jesus in the world is, of course, a distinctly Johannine emphasis. It should be noted that I John at this point bears a closer resemblance to Qumran than does the Gospel. In I John 4:6 we do have the contrast between "the spirit of truth" and "the spirit of error."

There is enough difference between the use of the expression "the spirit of truth" in Qumran and John to suggest independent lines of development. Both reflect some common Jewish heritage, but there is no evidence of direct influence from Qumran to John.

The importance of the Spirit in John. The Gospel of John makes it clear that at the time of writing, Jesus' promise of the Spirit has become a reality. The Spirit has now been given to the church. Consequently the writer seeks to instruct believers more fully regarding the importance, nature, and work of the Spirit.

Above all, the gift of the Spirit makes possible the presence of both the Father and the Son with the believer. Jesus says of the Father and of himself, "If a man loves me, . . . we will come to him and make our home with him" (14:23). The concept of the Spirit as the Presence of God is not a new idea. It finds expression in the Psalms in the following passages, where we have examples of Hebrew parallelism. Each line in the doublets has the same basic meaning. This is poetry and the second line repeats the thought expressed in the first.

> Cast me not away from thy presence,
> and take not thy holy Spirit from me.
> (Ps. 51:11)

> Whither shall I go from thy Spirit?
> Or whither shall I flee from thy presence?
> (Ps. 139:7)

In both examples the presence of God is equated with the Spirit of God. The Spirit is the presence of God as men experience that presence. What is distinct about John is that the Spirit is viewed as also making possible the continuing presence of Jesus (as well as of God the Father) with the believer. Furthermore, in the Old Testament the Spirit and God are equated. No distinction is made between them. The Holy Spirit is simply God as he is active in his world. We see the Spirit active, for example, in creation (Gen. 1:2). The Spirit anointed men for special ministry (Gen. 41:38; Judg. 6:34). Through the Spirit, men spoke for God (II Sam. 23:2; cf. II Peter 1:21). Despite the references in the Psalms, it is more normal for the Old Testament to think of the Spirit in relation to an unusual endowment for a specific duty or responsibility rather than as expressing the divine presence with the people of God on a day-by-day basis. This is much more a New Testament focus than it is an Old Testament one.

Furthermore, John's treatment of the Spirit makes a rather sharp difference between the Father and the Spirit (in a sense uncharacteristic of the Old Testament). By so doing, John helped to lay the foundation for the doctrine of the Trinity as it developed in later doctrinal discussions.

In addition to stressing the Spirit as the continuing presence of both the Father and the Son, John emphasizes the Spirit's work. Concerning the Spirit, John writes that when he comes he will convince the world of sin, of righteousness, and of judgment (16:8). The word rendered "convince" in the RSV carries the connotation "to prove guilty." The New English Bible uses the word "convict," which expresses the idea well. In this verse we are told that the Spirit will do three things:

1. He will prove that the world is guilty of sin, primarily the sin of refusing to believe in Jesus as the Christ.

2. The Spirit will also prove that the world was wrong about justice, for it will show that Jesus, whom the world declared to be guilty, was actually innocent and just.

3. Finally, he will demonstrate that in the very act of condemning Jesus the world itself is judged. By rejecting the light, the darkness of the world is manifested.

In 15:26–27 the Spirit's work of bearing witness is coupled with the statement that the disciples are to be witnesses. This coupling is not accidental, for the Spirit continues his work in and through believers. The Spirit bears witness and fulfills his mission through the believers, not independent of them. The Spirit ministers to and through the witnessing community. In this way the ministry that Jesus began continues in the world.[11]

Another promise concerning the Spirit which Jesus makes in the Fourth Gospel is that the Spirit will guide the disciples into all the truth (16:13). Does this mean new revelation? Not in the sense of new content.[12] A new understanding of what Jesus has done, however, and of who he is appears to be a major part of this further truth. Frequently we are told that some event in the life of Jesus was not fully understood until after Jesus' resurrection (2:22; 12:16; 13:7). These would be examples of the truth into which the Spirit guides the disciples. From John's perspective any further light brought by the Spirit must relate to Jesus Christ and must be in keeping with the foundational affirmation that in him the Father has revealed himself in the world. It is the Spirit's role to glorify the Son and to declare to the disciples truths concerning Jesus (16:14).

Having said the above, we must nonetheless recognize that John clearly goes beyond the words Jesus spoke during his earthly ministry. The author presents not only what Jesus said but adds much that is of the nature of his own understanding and interpretation of Jesus' works and words. The writer prepares his readers for this by quoting Jesus as saying that he had many things to say to them which they at that time were not prepared to receive. As a consequence some of these things they would receive through the Spirit rather than through Jesus (16:12 f.). It appears valid, therefore, to say that one function of the Paraclete doctrine in John is to give a defense for the validity of the deeper insights and understanding which the Fourth Gospel gives. The Paraclete, in other words, is both the source and the endorsement for the developed perspective on the life and ministry of Jesus contained in John. The author is a portrait painter. He is concerned to interpret, to give meaning, to set into perspective, the great events that had taken place. This he affirms he has done under the inspiration of the Spirit. He sees the promise of Jesus being fulfilled (at least in part) in his own work.

One of the reasons John may have put as much stress on the Spirit as he has was the disappointment felt by the church at the delay of the *parousia,* Christ's return. John is saying that Jesus has in a sense already returned to his church. He did not leave them as orphans but by the Spirit came back to be with them (14:18–23). The Lord is with his people through the Spirit. The believers are therefore to be about their assigned task of being witnesses to Jesus as the Christ, the Son of God. By this emphasis John counterbalanced the discouragement which some felt in the delay in Christ's return. Those with eyes of faith were urged to recognize that Jesus had indeed come back and was with them through the Spirit.

In a dramatic way there has developed a new interest in the Spirit in our generation. John's Gospel can be an aid in giving instruction on the primary work of the Spirit. John, for example, makes no reference to special charismatic gifts or special manifestations such as speaking in tongues. Some in our day argue that such things are the Spirit's primary work. In addition to Paul's words of caution in this regard, the Gospel of John can help put the focus on sound teaching, Christian love, obedience, ministry, and the Lordship of Christ. Since the Spirit speaks not concerning himself but concerning Jesus, it is proper to conclude that the Lordship of Christ in a believer's life is the clearest and primary evidence of a Spirit-led life.

12

〰〰〰〰〰〰〰〰〰〰〰〰〰〰〰〰〰〰

History and Interpretation

The historical accuracy of the Gospel of John has often been questioned. While some persons have maintained that the record of John is fully as factual as that found in Mark or one of the other Gospels, others have concluded that it is to be considered primarily as a theological work. As Bultmann has put it:

> The Gospel of John cannot be taken into account at all as a source for the teaching of Jesus.[1]

Mussner also expresses reservations about a literal approach to John. He writes:

> To what extent is the Johannine Christ "identical" with the historical Jesus of Nazareth? Should the *Vita Jesu* which the fourth evangelist presents not rather be termed (even if in an elevated sense) a novel about Jesus?[2]

The truth would appear to lie between the extremes of a literal approach and Bultmann's total rejection of John as a source for the teachings of Jesus. The recognition of firm historical roots behind the Fourth Gospel is receiving increas-

174

ing support among interpreters of this Gospel. As Raymond E. Brown has written:

> Within the material proper to John there is a strong element of historical plausibility, and . . . within the material shared by John and the Synoptics, John draws upon an independent and primitive tradition.[3]

C. H. Dodd in a very influential book has argued for a new appreciation of the historical tradition incorporated in the Fourth Gospel. He writes,

> For the more clearly the theological position of the Fourth Gospel is examined, the more clearly is it seen to involve a reference to history.[4]

In acknowledging this historical element, one must take care not to lose sight of the fact that John's Gospel does present the life and teachings of Jesus from a highly developed theological perspective. The Mussner quotation above brings this aspect of the Gospel to the forefront in a dramatic way. John is definitely a Gospel in which reflection and interpretation have played an extraordinary role. Whether or not the factual and interpretative materials can be separated with any satisfaction is a pressing question. There are scholars who are convinced that no such separation is possible. The factual and interpretative have been so intimately interwoven, in their judgment, that they must be dealt with as a unit and any attempt to separate them is destined to end in failure. As Hoskyns and Davey wrote:

> The theme of the Fourth Gospel is the non-historical that makes sense of history, the infinite that makes sense of time, God who makes sense of men and is therefore their Saviour. The specific technique of the author has been wrought out in order to grapple with this theme. For this reason, because the author has seen his theme so clearly, and held to it so consistently, it is impossible for the critic to separate what is

historical in the book from what is spiritual interpretation. To attempt to do so would be to misunderstand the theme altogether and to outrage the technique.[5]

John and the Synoptics. It is true that all of history involves interpretation and that any attempted separation between John and the Synoptic Gospels is artificial. Nevertheless, we do have the Synoptics before us with which we can compare the account given in The Gospel According to John. When we study the two together we soon notice that there are a number of noteworthy differences. Colwell and Titus[6] once made the comment that what others do for Jesus in the Synoptics, Jesus does for himself in John. In John, Jesus himself makes claims about his person and Messiahship which in the Synoptic Gospels are only gradually affirmed by a few of his more insightful disciples. Their confessions of his Messiahship come only about halfway through his ministry or later. In John nearly every title used of Jesus by the early church is addressed to him in the opening days of his ministry as recorded in the first chapter.

Similarly, the "I am" statements of John have no real parallel in the Synoptic Gospels. Taking this particular phenomenon as an example, we may well ask whether or not the repetitive "I am" formulas should not be attributed to a combination of the religious faith and the literary style of the author of the Gospel. Here we have a confession of faith in Jesus presented in the form of a first-person discourse. This is not to suggest that the statements are not accurate reflections of what the church then and now believes about our Lord, but it does mean that we should probably be wrong if we were to consider that these statements came in this particular form from Jesus himself. As Sanders and Mastin note correctly:

The teaching in the Fourth Gospel may be closer to that of Jesus in *substance* than has commonly been recognized, but its

form has very largely been imposed upon it by the evangelist,
or by the principal source from which he drew his material.[7]

Jesus' message has not only been transmitted in John, it has
been transformed. Leon Morris believes that in this transformation there was not a radical distortion of basic facts.
Therefore he writes:

> He did not have to distort his facts to accomplish his doctrinal
> aims. He was able to take what actually happened and speak
> of it in such a way as to bring out its deeper meaning. John
> was not trying to impose a pattern on the history, but to draw
> attention to the pattern that emerges from the history.[8]

Such literary freedom is a regular phenomenon in hymns
and in poetry. There is no need to reproach John for using
this method or style in presenting the message of our Lord.
We are dealing with a dramatic reformulation of the story of
Jesus. The author's central purpose was not primarily to add
new facts to what was already available to the community of
faith but rather to interpret more fully the meaning of Jesus
Christ, the Son of God. John seeks to make the message
concerning Jesus relevant for his own day and generation.
He interprets theologically the story of Jesus so that it will
have the most profound impact upon his own community.
The vital, pressing religious issues of the day helped to mold
his presentation. John's concept of the Spirit allowed him to
treat with freedom and creativity the traditions that had come
to him. These traditions he regarded as living and fluid rather
than static. John was part of an ongoing process that had
begun long before him. Mussner's comment seems to be
valid when he says:

> Consequently his interpretation of the figure of Christ is only
> the logical continuation of a process of interpretation which
> goes back much further.[9]

The element of interpretation runs throughout the entire

Gospel. It is clear in the first chapter both in the Logos doctrine and in the Christological affirmations which are there assembled. In the Book of Signs (chs. 2 to 12) the miracles are not treated for their own sake but as pointers to Jesus. They are interpreted Christologically. The events of the passion narrative are presented as fulfilling God's plan, and almost every detail is viewed as having theological significance. What about the discourses in John? Do they share the same interpretative quality?

The discourses. Few would argue that the discourses are verbatim reports. The style of John differs too markedly from that of the Synoptics to make this very plausible. Then, too, it has been correctly observed that the unique vocabulary found in the discourses of Jesus is consistent with the total narrative of this Gospel, including editorial comments. A very similar kind of vocabulary and emphasis is found in I John, where Jesus himself is, of course, not present. Consequently the conclusion cannot be escaped that in both John and I John the vocabulary and the style are the product of the creative writing of the author. Commenting on the fact that all the characters within the Fourth Gospel have the same style of speech, Strachan notes:

> This monotony of style indicates that the evangelist does not merely record, but interprets the teaching of Jesus as we know it from the Synoptic Gospels, imposing on it a characteristic Johannine idiom.[10]

In acknowledging the high degree to which John's own thought has entered into the telling of the Gospel story, we must remember that this process is also present in the writings of other New Testament authors as well. Sanders and Mastin write,

> The Marcan outline of Jesus' ministry is as much governed by dogmatic and theological considerations as is John's.[11]

As Leon Morris comments:

> The problem of history and the gospel is perhaps more acute in the case of the Fourth Gospel than in that of any of the other three. But it is essentially the same problem.[12]

The same phenomenon is also present in the writings of Paul. There is no evidence that Paul ever saw Jesus or heard him speak, and yet Paul, of all New Testament missionaries and writers, did most for the establishment of the church in the Mediterranean world. Once the churches were founded, he instructed them in Christian beliefs, Christian worship, Christian discipline, and church organization. He admits on one occasion that with regard to a specific question related to marriage he has no tradition handed down to him from "the Lord," that is, Jesus (I Cor. 7:12,25). He nevertheless goes on to give his own counsel in the matter and as he does so he confirms his personal conviction that in what he is sharing he reflects the mind of God. "And I think that I have the Spirit of God" (I Cor. 7:40), he writes. If through the years Christians had not acknowledged the validity of this claim by Paul, the writings of Paul would not have been admitted into the New Testament canon. Extending the same principle to John, can we deny to the author of the Fourth Gospel the right to freedom of religious expression under the guidance of the Spirit (John 16:12–15)? Is he not entitled to the same recognition of inspiration that is confidently granted to Paul? It is true that he has chosen to use the "Gospel" format for his teaching rather than letters, as Paul did. This does present something of a problem, since we are less prepared for the interpretative element here than we are when we read Paul's correspondence. We have seen, however, that the interpretative element in John differs only in degree from the same phenomenon which is recognized in the Synoptic Gospels. The best approach is not to decide ahead of time what the author of John should have done and then to censure him if he does not come up to our expectations. We might well ask ourselves to what extent our expectations are shaped by current literary practice. It is preferable to let John speak in the idiom of his choice and then interpret what he has written in the light of his intended purpose as stated in 20:30–31.

Barnabas Lindars draws a close analogy between the manner in which John uses the miracles creatively to fit his theological purpose and John's development of the discourses. He writes:

> The analogy of what John has done with the signs suggests that the discourses in which these are found are John's own compositions, in which he has used the sayings as the basis for very far-reaching developments. Just as the signs are traditional stories reworked by John for the purpose of his Gospel, so the discourses are traditional sayings expanded and developed with the same aim in view.[13]

Events, reflection, and the Spirit. In John's Gospel at least three elements have been closely interwoven. The interrelationship of these elements is very much a part of what is called "the problem of the Fourth Gospel." These three elements are:

1. Facts based on historical events in the life of Jesus.

2. Reflection, during several decades, upon the meaning of Jesus as the good news is preached, taught, and argued first in Palestine and then somewhere in the Diaspora.

3. The guidance of the Spirit which seems so definitely claimed by the author in 16:12–15. He appears to imply that by the Spirit's teaching, new understanding would come to the disciples after Jesus' departure, for they were not ready to receive it during Jesus' earthly ministry.

Through the interplay of these three elements there was developed the remarkable book we call The Gospel According to John. After much personal reflection, recognizing the guidance of the Spirit, the writer (or the one upon whom the writer depends for his material) felt free to apply definitive interpretations to events that had previously taken place. This was not going on in a vacuum, for the community in which the writer stood carried with it the traditions of the Christian church prior to its day. The pressing needs at the time of writing helped to determine what was selected for inclusion in the Gospel and what lessons were drawn from this selected and interpreted material.

The discourses as vehicles for theological presentation. The discourses focus on one central theme, namely, the person of Jesus Christ. This is also true of John's treatment of the "signs." Here the Fourth Gospel stands in marked contrast to the Synoptic Gospels. There Christ's miracles reflect his compassion primarily and are signs of the inauguration of the kingdom. They are not focused on Christology. Similarly the discourses in the Synoptics deal with a multitude of subjects, including ethics, the nature of the kingdom, and eschatology. Their form is sometimes proverbial, not unlike the maxims found in the book of Proverbs, as, for example, parts of the Sermon on the Mount. Parables of the kingdom are common. John's discourses have a distinctive quality about them. They move very rapidly from dialogue to monologue. They are best viewed as part of the literary style employed by the author for the presentation of theological instruction rather than as literal reports of actual discussions between Jesus and others. When Jesus' hearers speak, it is often for the purpose of providing opportunity for the discourses to continue to their intended conclusion. Disciples and others will ask questions or make statements that indicate various degrees of ignorance or misunderstanding. This prepares the way for a further elaboration of the thought of the discourse. This is a characteristic literary device of the author which serves as an effective medium for the communication of his message.

One suggestion that has been made, and that warrants

serious consideration, is that in the discourses in John we have material which is based upon and woven around key sayings of Jesus. The author, in other words, has not simply created his ideas. He has taken central concerns and emphases of Jesus and developed them. Dodd recognizes such a store of traditional sayings available to the author. He writes:

> It is clear that he had at his disposal a body of traditional sayings, parables, and dialogues, handed down separately or in formal sequences, which were drawn from the same general reservoir as those in the Synoptic Gospels, dealing with the same, or kindred, themes.[14]

Lindars suggests that one of the standard formulas used by John in reporting the words of Jesus "is a recurring sign that John is making use of a saying of Jesus from his stock of traditional material." [15] Lindars has reference to the solemn opening, "Amen, amen, I say to you." Lindars expands on this statement in his commentary when he writes:

> Synoptic-type sayings of Jesus have a far more important place in the structure of the Gospel than has been previously recognized. So far from being incidental to the Discourses, they are often the starting point of the whole argument. Very often John draws attention to this with the formula "Truly, truly, I say to you," which is not merely a stylistic device; in nearly every case it points to the use of a traditional saying.[16]

We would probably not be far wrong if we were to hold that the conversations between Jesus and the individuals mentioned in the Gospel of John actually took place, but that the recording of what was said and the manner in which the dialogues are developed should be attributed for the most part to the creative mind of the writer. The conversations are the framework for Johannine instruction. The author is desirous of expressing the message concerning Jesus as he understands it, and he feels himself under no duress to present verbatim reports. Because John stands some sixty years after the ministry of Jesus, such information was not available to him in any case. Quite apart from the problem of the preservation of such detailed interchange between Jesus and individuals is the matter of how reports on what was said when Jesus spoke privately with individuals like Nicodemus and the women of Samaria could have been secured. While a plea could be made that either Jesus or the one with whom Jesus spoke repeated what had taken place in a word-for-word report, the manner in which the themes of such conversations blend into the theology of the Fourth Gospel makes it preferable to see such conversations as a part of the literary style provided by the writer for the exposition of his theology. It is the significance of Jesus that concerned the writer, not just the words that he once spoke. He wishes to present the total impact of Jesus as the Son of God. This is why he is both highly selective and consistently theological in his presentation.

Sanders and Mastin compare the discourse material to expository preaching. They write:

> The clue to the understanding of the form of the Johannine teaching attributed to Jesus may be that the material in the Fourth Gospel consisted originally of sermons, preached by a man who was a Christian prophet, whose own words were as truly "words of the Lord" as those spoken by Jesus beside the sea of Galilee or in the Upper Room. In his sermons the prophet not only quoted what we mean by "the words of the Lord," but also paraphrased and adapted them.[17]

They make the further suggestion that the various feasts mentioned in John may be an indication of when such discourses were first prepared and delivered in the Johannine community.[18] They would then have been "timely" messages, closely synchronized with the festivals being celebrated in the nearby Jewish synagogues.

It is difficult to accept the above analysis, because we inevitably bring to our reading of this first-century literature a certain expectation and training that is the product of twentieth-century literary practice. In the reporting of news today, it is expected that quotation marks will be used whenever the exact words of a person are being reported. Similarly it is very improper to suggest that a person is being quoted exactly when this is not the case. Our laws of copyright, however, were not a part of first-century culture! Furthermore, we must remember that even in our day there is more than one literary style. In drama, for example, much greater freedom is allowed in telling the life story of an individual. We do not demand that the exact words of historical personages be repeated. It is the total effect of the drama that concerns us. The Gospel of John resembles a drama in many ways. J. Louis Martyn speaks of the account of the blind man receiving his sight in John, ch. 9, as "a *dramatic expansion* of the original miracle story." [19] Raymond E. Brown says of this incident, "We have here Johannine dramatic skill at its best." [20] He adds:

> A miracle story has been shaped into an ideal tool at the service of Christian apologetics and into an ideal instruction for those about to be baptized.[21]

Any failure to appreciate the dramatic element in John will result in making it more difficult to interpret what has taken place in the Fourth Gospel. Within a definite historical tradition, which is today increasingly appreciated, John gives his distinctive interpretation of the message and significance of Jesus.

Interpretation and truth. "Interpretation" must not be viewed as a word which, by its very denotation, implies a negative judgment about something. It does not and should not carry the connotation of "misinterpretation." As John interprets the gospel, it is his intent to draw out the latent but essential implications of the story of Jesus. He was helping his readers to see more clearly what it all meant and he was concerned to apply it to contemporary issues. The facts without the meaning would be for him without significance. Since he has the needs of his intended readers primarily in view, he does not hesitate to make the discourses the vehicles for applying the words of Jesus to them in their time and place. Note the interesting parallel to this in the manner in which the risen Christ speaks to the churches of Asia Minor in terms of *their* specific weaknesses, strengths, trials, and needs in the book of Revelation, chs. 2 and 3. In much the same way John's Gospel appears to make no clear distinction between what was said by Jesus while he was on earth and what, through the Spirit, he *now* says to the church as it faces persecution, false teaching, and religious controversy.

While "meaning" was also very much a concern of the writers of the Synoptic Gospels, it is valid to say that in the case of The Gospel According to John the element of theological interpretation is more consciously, consistently, and forcefully present. It completely permeates the purpose and contents of the Gospel. It is the very dominance of this quality which makes the Fourth Gospel stand in such a sharp contrast to the other three.

The analysis of The Gospel According to John which is here presented differs in two important respects from the view that John is strictly a theological restatement of the gospel without concern for historical roots and without any defensible claim for historical credibility:

1. This approach assumes an independent historical tradition which has been preserved in The Gospel According to John and which is in some ways parallel to the tradition reflected in the Synoptic Gospels. The result is that John cannot be ignored in the study of the life and actions of Jesus. There are times when information contained in John can

properly be viewed as supplementing and, on occasion, correcting that found in the Synoptic Gospels.

2. There appears to exist in each and every miracle and discourse that is recorded in John a historical kernel which the author has preserved from his tradition and around which he builds his theological exposition. The big question remains of how this kernel is to be recognized and, if possible, separated from the homily in which it is embedded. Some would maintain that the historical tradition has been so modified that the task of recovering it is impossible. Hoskyns and Davey felt that the effort to analyze John into fact and interpretation is both improper and beyond possibility.[22] Not all interpreters of the Fourth Gospel share this judgment. Among those who have contributed significantly to an effort to recover the historical tradition behind the Fourth Gospel is C. H. Dodd.[23] It can be expected that this area of debate will receive increased scholarly attention in the years immediately ahead.

Notes

CHAPTER 1. JOHN SPEAKS TO OUR WORLD

1. Rudolf Bultmann, *The Gospel of John*, pp. 466 f., 474 f., and Raymond E. Brown, *The Gospel According to John*, Vol. I, p. 562.
2. C. H. Dodd, *The Interpretation of the Fourth Gospel*, p. 9.
3. W. C. van Unnik, "The Purpose of St. John's Gospel," in *Studia Evangelica*, Vol. I, p. 410.
4. C. K. Barrett, *The Gospel According to St. John*, p. 115.
5. E. Hoskyns and F. N. Davey, *The Fourth Gospel*, 2d ed., p. 159.
6. R. E. Brown, *The Gospel According to John*, Vol. I, pp. lxxiii, lxxviii.
7. John 1:38,41; 6:4.
8. See the discussion in J. Louis Martyn, *History and Theology in the Fourth Gospel*, pp. 36 ff.
9. Eusebius, *Ecclesiastical History*, VI. xiv. Loeb Classical Library. English tr. by J. E. L. Oulton. (Harvard University Press, 1942 [1932].)
10. See the discussion on this in R. E. Brown, *The Gospel According to John*, Vol. I, pp. xxxii–xxxix.

CHAPTER 2. LIFE!

1. Franz Mussner, "*Zōē*. Die Anschauung vom 'Leben' im vierten Evangelium unter Berücksichtigung der Johannesbriefe," *Münchener Theologische Studien,* Vol. 1, No. 5 (1952), pp. v–xv, 1–190.

2. Floyd V. Filson, "The Gospel of Life," in W. Klassen and G. F. Snyder (eds.), *Current Issues in New Testament Interpretation,* pp. 111–123.

3. E. Smilde, *Leven in de Johanneïsche Geschriften,* pp. 260, 264. (Translation mine.)

4. Alf Correll, *Consummatum Est,* p. 108.

5. C. K. Barrett, "The Place of Eschatology in the Fourth Gospel," *Expository Times,* Vol. 59 (1947–1948), p. 305.

6. C. K. Barrett, *The Gospel According to St. John,* p. 58.

7. Mussner, "*Zōē*," *loc. cit.,* p. 184.

8. *Ibid.,* pp. 145–147.

9. U. E. Simon, "Eternal Life in the Fourth Gospel," in F. L. Cross (ed.), *Studies in the Fourth Gospel,* p. 103.

10. R. Schnackenburg, *The Gospel According to St. John,* Vol. I, p. 160.

11. *Ibid.*

12. R. Schnackenburg, "Der Gedanke des Lebens im Joh-Ev," Exkurs 12 in his *Das Johannesevangelium,* Vol. II, pp. 438–439. (Translation mine.)

CHAPTER 3. JESUS AS THE WORD

1. See discussion in E. M. Sidebottom, *The Christ of the Fourth Gospel,* p. 194.

2. See discussion in Schnackenburg, *The Gospel According to St. John,* Vol. I, pp. 154 ff.

3. W. H. Cadman, *The Open Heaven,* ed. by G. B. Caird, p. 28.

4. See Oscar Cullmann, *The Christology of the New Testament,* p. 186.

5. Ernst Käsemann, "The Structure and Purpose of the Pro-

logue to John's Gospel," in his *New Testament Questions of Today,*
pp. 158, 159, 161.

6. E. C. Colwell and E. L. Titus, *The Gospel of the Spirit,*
pp. 73–74.

7. Cullmann, *The Christology of the New Testament,* p. 256.

8. H. Conzelmann, *An Outline of the Theology of the New
Testament,* p. 334.

9. Bultmann, *The Gospel of John,* p. 24.

10. Joachim Jeremias, *Der Prolog des Johannesevangeliums,* p. 27.

11. S. Schultz, *Komposition und Herkunft der johanneischen
Reden,* p. 31; Barnabas Lindars, *Behind the Fourth Gospel,* p. 74;
Sidebottom, *The Christ of the Fourth Gospel,* pp. 203–207.

12. Dodd, *The Interpretation of the Fourth Gospel,* p. 275.

13. T. E. Pollard, *Johannine Christology and the Early Church,* pp.
6–7,

14. R. E. Brown, *The Gospel According to John,* Vol. I, pp. cxxiv,
523.

15. Jack T. Sanders, *The New Testament Christological Hymns,*
Ch. 2, "The Prologue of John."

16. Lorenz Durr, *Die Wertung des göttlichen Wortes im Alten
Testament und im antiken Orient,* pp. 158 ff.

17. Jack T. Sanders, *The New Testament Christological Hymns,*
p. 50.

18. Helmer Ringgren, *Word and Wisdom. Studies in the Hypostatization of Divine Qualities and Functions in the Ancient Near East.*

19. *Ibid.,* p. 157.

20. Jack T. Sanders, *The New Testament Christological Hymns,*
p. 56.

21. J. Rendel Harris, *The Origin of the Prologue to St. John's
Gospel,* p. 6.

22. Bultmann, *The Gospel of John,* p. 18.

23. Schnackenburg, *The Gospel According to St. John,* Vol. I, pp.
226 ff.

24. Käsemann, *New Testament Questions of Today,* p. 150.

25. Barrett, *The Gospel According to St. John,* p. 126. He
develops this position more fully in *The Prologue of St. John's Gospel.*

26. Robert M. Grant, *A Historical Introduction to the New
Testament,* p. 159.

CHAPTER 4. OTHER TITLES FOR JESUS

1. Cullmann, *The Christology of the New Testament,* p. 186.

2. Ernst Käsemann, *The Testament of Jesus,* p. 13.

3. A. J. B. Higgins, *Jesus and the Son of Man,* pp. 153–184.

4. Käsemann, *The Testament of Jesus,* p. 10.

5. Schnackenburg, *The Gospel According to St. John,* Vol. I, p. 532.

6. Martyn, *History and Theology in the Fourth Gospel,* p. 132.

7. Cadman, *The Open Heaven,* p. 33.

8. E. D. Freed, "The Son of Man in the Fourth Gospel," *Journal of Biblical Literature,* Vol. 86 (1967), pp. 402–409.

9. I. H. Marshall, "The Divine Sonship of Jesus," *Interpretation,* Vol. 21 (1967), p. 88.

10. Cullmann, *The Christology of the New Testament,* p. 303.

11. E. Schweizer, *"Huios," TDNT,* Vol. VIII, p. 387.

12. J. Coutts, "The Messianic Secret in St. John's Gospel," in *Studia Evangelica,* Vol. III, p. 53.

13. W. F. Lofthouse, "Fatherhood and Sonship in the Fourth Gospel," *Expository Times,* Vol. 43 (1931–1932), p. 447. This idea is discussed further in his book *The Father and the Son: A Study in Johannine Thought* (London: SCM Press, Ltd., 1934).

14. Schnackenburg, *Das Johannesevangelium,* Vol. II, p. 151.

15. *Ibid.,* p. 167. (Translation mine.)

16. G. Schrenk, *"Patēr," TDNT,* Vol. V, pp. 998, 999.

17. Dale Moody, "God's Only Son: The Translation of John 3:16 in the Revised Standard Version," *Journal of Biblical Literature,* Vol. 72 (1953), p. 213.

18. *Ibid.,* p. 217.

19. F. Büchsel, *"Monogenēs," TDNT,* Vol. IV, p. 741, f.n. 20.

20. Leon Morris, *The Gospel According to John,* pp. 105, 106. Cf. R. E. Brown, *The Gospel According to John,* Vol. I, p. 13.

21. See Sidebottom, *The Christ of the Fourth Gospel,* p. 154.

22. W. Manson, "The *EGO EIMI* of the Messianic Presence in the New Testament," *Journal of Theological Studies,* Vol. 48 (1947), p. 141.

23. Philip B. Harner, *The "I am" of the Fourth Gospel,* p. 60.

24. R. E. Brown, *The Gospel According to John,* Vol. I, p. 537; Barrett, *The Gospel According to St. John,* p. 283; Dodd, *The Interpretation of the Fourth Gospel,* p. 95; André Feuillet, "Les *Ego eimi* christologiques du quatrième évangile," *Recherches de Science Religieuse,* Vol. 54 (1966), p. 235.

25. Harner, *The "I am" of the Fourth Gospel,* p. 29.

26. Schnackenburg, *Das Johannesevangelium,* Vol. II, p. 65. (Translation mine.)

27. Bultmann, *The Gospel of John,* p. 225, n. 3.

28. E. Schweizer, *Ego Eimi.*

29. H. Zimmermann, "Das absolute *Ego eimi* als die neutestamentliche Offenbarungsformel," *Biblische Zeitschrift,* Vol. 4 (1960), pp. 271–276.

30. Feuillet, "Les *Ego eimi* christologiques du quatrième évangile," *loc. cit.,* pp. 235–240.

31. Harner, *The "I am" of the Fourth Gospel,* p. 65.

32. Lindars, *Behind the Fourth Gospel,* p. 72. See also R. E. Brown, *The Gospel According to John,* Vol. I, pp. 537, 538.

33. Schnackenburg, *Das Johannesevangelium,* Vol. II, p. 67. (Translation mine.)

34. *Ibid.* Cf. George W. MacRae, "The Ego-Proclamation in Gnostic Sources," in E. Bammel (ed.), *The Trial of Jesus,* pp. 122–134.

35. Schnackenburg, *Das Johannesevangelium,* Vol. II, p. 69. (Translation mine.)

36. E. Stauffer, *Jesus and His Story,* p. 192.

37. *Ibid.,* p. 193.

38. R. E. Brown, *The Gospel According to John,* Vol. I, p. 538. Cf. Schnackenburg, *Das Johannesevangelium,* Vol. II, pp. 67–69.

CHAPTER 5. THE CHILDREN OF GOD

1. See Severino Pancaro, " 'People of God' in St. John's Gospel?" *New Testament Studies* 16 (1969–1970), pp. 114–129.

2. For an excellent discussion see the article by Severino Pancaro cited above.

3. Rudolf Bultmann, *Theology of the New Testament,* Vol. II, p. 92.

4. Bultmann, *The Gospel of John*, pp. 367 ff.

5. Dodd, *The Interpretation of the Fourth Gospel*, p. 123.

6. N. A. Dahl, "The Johannine Church and History," in W. Klassen and G. F. Snyder (eds.), *Current Issues in New Testament Interpretation*, pp. 136 f.

7. Oscar Cullmann, "L'Evangile johannique et l'histoire du salut," *New Testament Studies*, Vol. 11 (1964–1965), pp. 111–122.

8. Dan O. Via, Jr., "Darkness, Christ, and the Church in the Fourth Gospel," *Scottish Journal of Theology*, Vol. 14 (1961), p. 173. The same position is argued by F. J. A. Hort, *The Christian Ecclesia*, p. 30; E. F. Scott, *The Fourth Gospel: Its Purpose and Theology*, 2d ed., p. 137; and Barrett, *The Gospel According to St. John*, p. 79.

9. I am indebted for this phrase to Raymond E. Brown in a lecture given at Eastern Baptist Theological Seminary, Philadelphia, on March 22, 1974.

10. *Ibid.*

11. R. E. Brown, *The Gospel According to John*, Vol. II, pp. 598–601, 744.

12. *Ibid.*, p. 776.

13. E. Schweizer, *Church Order in the New Testament*, p. 130.

14. *Ibid.*, p. 124.

15. E. Schweizer, "The Concept of the Church in the Gospel and Epistles of St. John," in A. J. B. Higgins (ed.), *New Testament Essays*, p. 237.

16. *Ibid.*, p. 240.

17. Bultmann, *Theology of the New Testament*, Vol. II, p. 91.

18. *Ibid.*

19. N. A. Dahl, "The Johannine Church and History" in Klassen and Snyder (eds.), *Current Issues in New Testament Interpretation*, pp. 124–142.

20. R. Schnackenburg, *The Church in the New Testament*, p. 103.

21. *Ibid.*, p. 104.

22. *Ibid.*, p. 105.

23. Schnackenburg, *The Gospel According to St. John*, Vol. I, p. 163.

24. C. F. D. Moule, "The Individualism of the Fourth Gospel," *Novum Testamentum*, Vol. 5 (1962), p. 185.

25. Ernst Käsemann, *New Testament Questions of Today*, p. 255

("Unity and Multiplicity in the New Testament Doctrine of the Church").

26. Käsemann, *The Testament of Jesus*, p. 37.

27. *Ibid.*, p. 39.

28. R. E. Brown, *The Gospel According to John*, Vol. I, p. cix.

29. Raymond E. Brown, "The Kerygma of the Gospel According to John: The Johannine View of Jesus in Modern Studies," *Interpretation*, Vol. 21 (1967), p. 392.

30. Bultmann, *The Gospel of John*, p. 472.

31. E. Schweizer, "Das johanneische Zeugnis vom Herrenmahl," *Evangelische Theologie*, Vol. 12 (1952 1953), pp. 341 363.

32. G. H. C. Macgregor, *The Gospel of John*, p. xxx.

33. *Ibid.*

34. For a detailed study of the controversy between synagogue and church as reflected in the Fourth Gospel, see the study by Martyn, *History and Theology in the Fourth Gospel*.

35. Colwell and Titus, *The Gospel of the Spirit*, pp. 51, 52.

36. O. Cullmann, *Early Christian Worship*, p. 95.

37. Raymond E. Brown, *New Testament Essays*, pp. 120–122 ("The Eucharist and Baptism in John").

38. R. E. Brown, *The Gospel According to John*, Vol. II, pp. 701, 702.

39. Martyn, *History and Theology in the Fourth Gospel*, pp. 39 ff.; Barrett, *The Gospel According to St. John*, pp. 299, 300; Hoskyns and Davey, *The Fourth Gospel*, 2d ed., p. 356. On the other hand Morris, in *The Gospel According to John*, prefers to interpret the excommunication as related to the time of Jesus (pp. 488, 489).

CHAPTER 6. BELIEVE

1. R. E. Brown, *The Gospel According to John*, Vol. I, p. 513.

2. For further discussion see Dodd, *The Interpretation of the Fourth Gospel*, p. 183.

3. Bultmann, *The Theology of the New Testament*, Vol. II, pp. 71 f.

4. H. Schlier, *Besinnung auf das Neue Testament*, p. 280.

5. *Ibid.*, p. 281. (Translation mine.)

6. G. L. Phillips, "Faith and Vision in the Fourth Gospel," in F. L. Cross (ed.), *Studies in the Fourth Gospel,* p. 91.

7. Bultmann, *The Theology of the New Testament,* Vol. II, p. 72. Cf. R. E. Brown, *The Gospel According to John,* Vol. I, pp. 501–503.

8. *Ibid.*

9. A. Schlatter, *Der Glaube im Neuen Testament,* p. 216.

10. H. Wenz, "Sehen und Glauben bei Johannes," *Theologische Zeitschrift,* Vol. 17 (1961), pp. 17–25.

11. R. Bultmann, *"Ginōskō," TDNT,* Vol. I, p. 712. See also Dodd, *The Interpretation of the Fourth Gospel,* pp. 184, 185.

12. Bultmann, *The Theology of the New Testament,* Vol. II, p. 73.

13. Schnackenburg, *The Gospel According to St. John,* Vol. I, p. 566.

14. H. Schlier, *Besinnung auf das Neue Testament,* p. 293. (Translation mine.)

15. Mussner, *"Zōē," loc. cit.,* p. 95. *("Die entschlossene, vollkommene und vertrauensvolle Hinwendung der ganzen Person mit all ihren Kraften zu Jesus.")*

CHAPTER 7. KNOW

1. I. de la Potterie, *"Oida* et *ginōskō.* Les Deux Modes de la connaissance dans le quatrième évangile." *Biblica,* Vol. 40 (1959), p. 709.

2. R. P. Casey, "Gnosis, Gnosticism, and the New Testament," in W. D. Davies and D. Daube (eds.), *The Background of the New Testament and Its Eschatology,* p. 74.

3. I. de la Potterie, *"Oida et ginōskō," loc. cit.,* pp. 709–725. Also E. K. Lee, *The Religious Thought of St. John,* pp. 233, 234.

4. R. E. Brown, *The Gospel According to John,* Vol. I, p. 514.

5. Bultmann, *"Ginōskō,"* in *TDNT,* Vol. I, p. 689.

6. *Ibid.,* p. 692.

7. P. Bonnard, "Connaître Dieu selon le quatrième évangile et la gnose hellénistique," *Foi et Vie,* Vol. 64 (1965), pp. 484–488.

8. See discussion in Lee, *The Religious Thought of St. John,* p. 233, and in Barrett, *The Gospel According to St. John,* p. 136.

9. Jer. 31:31–34.

10. M. Casalis, "Le Thème de la connaissance de Dieu dans les milieux littéraires essénien, paulinien et johannique," *Foi et Vie,* Vol. 64 (1965), pp. 518, 519.

11. Bultmann, *Theology of the New Testament,* Vol. II, pp. 73, 74.

12. Dodd, *The Interpretation of the Fourth Gospel,* p. 169.

13. John 14:21,23. See Dodd, *The Interpretation of the Fourth Gospel,* pp. 199, 200.

14. See C. K. Barrett, "The Theological Vocabulary of the Fourth Gospel and of the Gospel of Truth," in Klassen and Snyder (eds.), *Current Issues in New Testament Interpretation,* pp. 210–223; R. E. Brown, "The Gospel of Thomas and St. John's Gospel," *New Testament Studies,* Vol. 9 (1962–1963), pp. 155–177.

15. See discussion in Schnackenburg, *The Gospel According to St John,* Vol. I, p. 549.

16. H. C. Puech and others, *The Jung Codex: A Newly Recovered Gnostic Papyrus,* tr. and ed. by F. L. Cross, pp. 13 ff.

17. R. McL. Wilson, "Gnostic Origins," *Vigiliae Christianae,* Vol. 9 (November, 1955), pp. 193–211.

18. Dodd, *The Interpretation of the Fourth Gospel,* p. 98.

19. Wilson, "Gnostic Origins," *loc. cit.,* p. 204.

20. C. H. Dodd, *The Bible and the Greeks,* p. 248.

21. Schnackenburg, *The Gospel According to St. John,* Vol. I, p. 549.

22. R. Schnackenburg, "Häretische Gnosis und christliches 'Gotterkennen,' " Exkurs 3 in his *Die Johannesbriefe,* pp. 95–101.

23. Barrett, *The Gospel According to St. John,* p. 68.

24. Casey, "Gnosis, Gnosticism, and the New Testament," *loc. cit.,* p. 73.

25. Floyd V. Filson, "The Gospel of Life," in Klassen and Snyder (eds.), *Current Issues in New Testament Interpretation,* p. 117.

26. These conclusions are discussed at greater length in my dissertation "A Comparative Study of Certain Alleged Similarities Between the Literature of Qumran and the Fourth Gospel." (Unpublished dissertation. University of Southern California, 1959.)

27. W. D. Davies, " 'Knowledge' in the Dead Sea Scrolls and Matthew 11:25–30," *Harvard Theological Review,* Vol. 46 (July, 1953), p. 135, n. 74.

28. Millar Burrows, *The Dead Sea Scrolls,* p. 259.

29. F. F. Bruce, *Second Thoughts on the Dead Sea Scrolls,* p. 104.
30. Dodd, *The Interpretation of the Fourth Gospel,* p. 102.

CHAPTER 8. LOVE

1. Victor Paul Furnish, *The Love Command in the New Testament,* p. 151.
2. G. Schrenk, *"Entolē," TDNT,* Vol. II, p. 553.
3. R. Percival Brown, *"Entolē Kainē* (St. John 13:34)," *Theology,* Vol. 26 (April, 1933) p. 191. A very similar position is taken in a helpful discussion by Lee, *The Religious Thought of St. John,* pp. 244–250.
4. R. E. Brown, *The Gospel According to John,* Vol. II, p. 614.
5. G. Quell and others, *"Agapaō," TDNT,* Vol. I, p. 27.
6. E. Stauffer, in Quell and others, *"Agapaō," TDNT,* Vol. I, p. 35.
7. E. Evans, "The Verb *agapan* in the Fourth Gospel," in F. L. Cross (ed.), *Studies in the Fourth Gospel,* p. 69.
8. Stauffer, in Quell and others, *"Agapaō," loc. cit.,* p. 37.
9. *Ibid.,* p. 39.
10. C. Spicq, *Agape in the New Testament,* Vol. III, p. 19.
11. W. Hendriksen, *Exposition of the Gospel According to John,* Vol. II, pp. 494–500.
12. E. Evans, "The Verb *agapan* in the Fourth Gospel," *loc. cit.,* p. 70.
13. Morris, *The Gospel According to John,* p. 871, f.n. 39.
14. Bultmann, *The Gospel of John,* p. 711, f.n. 5. R. E. Brown in *The Gospel According to John,* Vol. II, pp. 1102–1103, comes to the same conclusion.
15. Käsemann, *The Testament of Jesus,* p. 59.
16. *Ibid.,* p. 60.
17. C. R. Bowen, "Love in the Fourth Gospel," *Journal of Religion,* Vol. 13 (1933), p. 46.
18. W. F. Howard, *Christianity According to St. John,* p. 170.
19. Paul Wernle, *The Beginnings of Christianity,* Vol. II, pp. 336, 337.

CHAPTER 9. LIGHT AND DARKNESS

1. W. H. Cadman, *The Open Heaven: The Revelation of God in the Johannine Sayings of Jesus,* ed. by G. B. Caird, pp. 26, 27.
2. Schnackenburg, *The Gospel According to St. John,* Vol. I, pp. 366, 367, and *Das Johannesevangelium,* Vol. II, p. 435, f.n. 3.
3. See Eric L. Titus, *The Message of the Fourth Gospel,* p. 59.
4. See Barrett, *The Gospel According to St. John,* p. 137.
5. Titus, *The Message of the Fourth Gospel,* p. 95
6. R. E. Brown, *New Testament Essays,* p. 160 ("The Qumran Scrolls and the Johannine Gospel and Epistles"); also in his *The Gospel According to John,* Vol. I, p. 516
7. 1QS 3:18,19. Note that 1QS is the symbol commonly used to designate the Manual of Discipline.
8. 1QS 3:19,20. The quotations from the Manual of Discipline are from W. H. Brownlee's translation. See W. H. Brownlee, "The Dead Sea Manual of Discipline: Translation and Notes," *Bulletin of the American Schools of Oriental Research,* Supplementary Studies, Nos. 10–12. New Haven: American Schools of Oriental Research, 1951.
9. 1QS 3:21–23.
10. 1QS 3:24,25.
11. 1QS 3:25; 4:1,18.
12. 1QS 4:2.
13. 1QS 4:9–11.
14. 1QS 4:16–19.
15. *Ibid.*
16. Habakkuk Commentary, Col. VII, 10–14.
17. The War Rule, Col. I. (Translation from G. Vermès, *The Dead Sea Scrolls in English.*)
18. The Hymns, Col. IV. (G. Vermès' translation.)
19. 1QS 11:12.
20. K. G. Kuhn, "New Light on Temptation, Sin and Flesh in the New Testament," in Krister Stendahl (ed.), *The Scrolls and the New Testament,* p. 98.
21. R. E. Brown, *New Testament Essays* ("The Qumran Scrolls and the Johannine Gospel and Epistles"), p. 143.

22. Colwell and Titus, *The Gospel of the Spirit*, p. 155.

23. J. H. Charlesworth, "A Critical Comparison of the Dualism in 1QS III, 13–IV,26 and the 'Dualism' Contained in the Fourth Gospel," in J. H. Charlesworth (ed.), *John and Qumran*, p. 98.

24. *Ibid.,* p. 93.

25. James L. Price, "Light from Qumran Upon Some Aspects of Johannine Theology," in J. H. Charlesworth (ed.), *John and Qumran*, p. 21.

26. I John 3:7–10; 4:1–6.

27. See Price, "Light from Qumran," *loc. cit.,* p. 22.

28. J. N. Sanders, *A Commentary on the Gospel According to St. John*, p. 22.

29. J. N. Sanders, "John, Gospel of," in *The Interpreter's Dictionary of the Bible*, Vol. E-J, p. 938.

30. Colwell and Titus, *The Gospel of the Spirit*, pp. 154, 155.

31. *Ibid.,* p. 155.

32. The Testaments of the Twelve Patriarchs, Testament of Judah 20:1. (Translation by R. H. Charles, in R. H. Charles [ed.], *The Apocrypha and Pseudepigrapha of the Old Testament in English*, Vol. II.)

33. The Testaments of the Twelve Patriarchs, Testament of Asher 1:3-9. (R. H. Charles' translation.)

34. The Epistle of Barnabas, 18:1. (Translation from Robert A. Kraft, *Barnabas and the Didache*.)

35. The Shepherd of Hermas, Mandate VI. (Translation from Graydon F. Snyder, *The Shepherd of Hermas*.)

36. W. D. Davies, "Paul and the Dead Sea Scrolls: Flesh and Spirit," in Krister Stendahl (ed.), *The Scrolls and the New Testament*, p. 157.

CHAPTER 10. TRUTH

1. H. G. Liddell and R. Scott, *A Greek-English Lexicon*, p. 63.

2. Dodd, *The Interpretation of the Fourth Gospel*, p. 173.

3. F. Brown, S. R. Driver, and C. A. Briggs, *A Hebrew and English Lexicon of the Old Testament*, p. 54.

4. Dodd, *The Interpretation of the Fourth Gospel*, p. 173.

5. F. Büchsel, *Der Begriff der Wahrheit in dem Evangelium und den Briefen des Johannes.*

6. Scott, *The Fourth Gospel: Its Purpose and Theology*, 2d ed., p. 253.

7. Dodd, *The Interpretation of the Fourth Gospel*, p. 174.

8. *Ibid.*, p. 177, 178.

9. Howard, *Christianity According to St. John*, p. 184.

10. *Ibid.*, p. 185. Cf. R. Bultmann, *"Alētheia," TDNT*, Vol. I, pp. 232 ff.

11. Yrjö Alanen, "Das Wahrheitsproblem in der Bibel und in der griechischen Philosophie," *Kerygma und Dogma*, Vol. 3 (1957), pp. 230–239.

12. I. de la Potterie, "L'Arrière-fond du thème johannique de vérité," in *Studia Evangelica*, Vol. I, pp. 277 294. See also S. Aalen, "'Truth,' a Key Word in St. John's Gospel," *Studia Evangelica*, Vol. II, pp. 3–24.

13. Josef Blank, "Der johanneische Wahrheits-Begriff," *Biblische Zeitschrift*, Vol. 7 (1963), pp. 163–173.

14. Schnackenburg, *Das Johannesevangelium*, Vol. II, pp. 265–281.

15. Alf Corell, *Consummatum Est*, p. 161.

16. See R. E. Brown, *The Gospel According to John*, Vol. II, p. 630.

17. See R. E. Brown, *The Gospel According to John*, Vol. I, pp. 500, 501.

18. Bultmann, *The Gospel of John*, p. 364.

19. Cf. R. E. Brown, *The Gospel According to John*, Vol. I, p. 180.

20. Freed, "The Manner of Worship in John 4:32 f." in *Search the Scriptures*, ed. J. M. Myers *et al.*, pp. 33–48; R. Schnackenburg, "Die 'Anbetung in Geist und Wahrheit' (Joh 4:23) im Lichte von Qumran-Texten," *Biblische Zeitschrift*, Vol. 3 (1959), pp. 88–94.

21. 1QS 1:5; 5:3.

22. Gen. 47:29; Josh. 2:14; Judg. 9:16, 19; II Sam. 2:6; II Chron. 31:20; Neh. 9:33; Ps. 111:8.

23. Cf. G. A. Koch, "An Investigation of the Possible Relationship Between the Gospel of John and the Sectarian Documents of the Dead Sea Scrolls." Unpublished thesis. Philadelphia: Eastern Baptist Theological Seminary, 1959. Pp. 41 ff.

24. Cf. R. E. Brown, *The Gospel According to John*, Vol. I, p. 500.

CHAPTER 11. THE SPIRIT OF TRUTH

1. Franz Mussner, "Die johanneischen Parakletsprüche und die apostolische Tradition," *Biblische Zeitschrift*, Vol. 5 (1961), pp. 56–70.

2. See Bruce Vawter, "Johannine Theology," in R. E. Brown and others (eds.), *The Jerome Biblical Commentary*, pp. 828–839; especially section 41 on p. 836.

3. *The Gospel of the Spirit* is the title given by E. C. Colwell and E. L. Titus to their book on the Gospel of John.

4. In *Pirqe Aboth* iv, 11 (second century A.D.). Cited by R. E. Brown, *The Gospel According to John*, Vol. II, p. 1136.

5. R. E. Brown, "The Paraclete in the Fourth Gospel," *New Testament Studies*, Vol. 13 (1966–1967), p. 119.

6. Bultmann, *The Gospel of John*, pp. 566–572.

7. S. Mowinckel, "Die Vorstellungen des Spätjudentums vom heiligen Geist als Fürsprecher und der johanneische Paraklet," *Zeitschrift für die Neutestamentliche Wissenschaft*, Vol. 32 (1933), pp. 97–130; F. M. Cross, *The Ancient Library of Qumran and Modern Biblical Studies*, pp. 159, 160; George Johnston, *The Spirit-Paraclete in the Gospel of John*, pp. 92 ff.

8. R. E. Brown, *The Gospel According to John*, Vol. II, pp. 1137–1139.

9. *Ibid.*, pp. 1139–1141.

10. A. R. C. Leaney, "The Johannine Paraclete and the Qumran Scrolls," in J. H. Charlesworth (ed.), *John and Qumran*, pp. 38–61.

11. See C. K. Barrett, "The Holy Spirit in the Fourth Gospel," *Journal of Theological Studies*, N.S., Vol. 1 (1950), pp. 14,15.

12. See Ernst Bammel, "Jesus und der Paraklet in Johannes 16," in B. Lindars and S. S. Smalley (eds.), *Christ and Spirit in the New Testament*, pp. 199–217.

CHAPTER 12. HISTORY AND INTERPRETATION

1. Rudolf Bultmann, *Jesus and the Word*, p. 12.

2. Franz Mussner, *The Historical Jesus in the Gospel of St. John*, p. 7.

3. R. E. Brown, *The Gospel According to John*, Vol. I, p. xlviii.

4. C. H. Dodd, *Historical Tradition in the Fourth Gospel*, p. 4.

5. Hoskyns and Davey, *The Fourth Gospel*, 2d ed., pp. 129–130.

6. Colwell and Titus, *The Gospel of the Spirit*, p. 32.

7. Sanders and Mastin, *A Commentary on the Gospel According to John*, pp. 15–16.

8. Leon Morris, "History and Theology in the Fourth Gospel," in *Faith and Thought*, Vol. 92 (1962), p. 125.

9. Mussner, *The Historical Jesus in the Gospel of St. John*, p. 73.

10. R. H. Strachan, *The Fourth Gospel: Its Significance and Environment*, 3d ed., p. 15.

11. Sanders and Mastin, *A Commentary on the Gospel According to John*, p. 17.

12. Leon Morris, *Studies in the Fourth Gospel*, pp. 78, 79.

13. Barnabas Lindars, *Behind the Fourth Gospel*, p. 41.

14. Dodd, *Historical Tradition in the Fourth Gospel*, p. 430.

15. Lindars, *Behind the Fourth Gospel*, p. 44.

16. Barnabas Lindars, *The Gospel of John*, p. 48. A. M. Hunter has listed and discussed these Synoptic-type sayings in his *According to John*, Chs. 8 and 9.

17. Sanders and Mastin, *A Commentary on the Gospel According to John*, p. 16.

18. *Ibid.*

19. Martyn, *History and Theology in the Fourth Gospel*, p. 5.

20. R. E. Brown, *The Gospel According to John*, Vol. I, p. 376.

21. *Ibid.*, p. 378.

22. Hoskyns and Davey, *The Fourth Gospel*, 2d ed., pp. 34, 35.

23. Dodd, *Historical Tradition in the Fourth Gospel*.

Bibliography

PART I. TITLES IN ENGLISH

Aalen, S., " 'Truth,' a Key Word in St. John's Gospel," *Studia Evangelica*, Vol. II. Berlin: Akademie-Verlag, 1964. Pp. 3–24.

Achtemeier, E., "Jesus Christ, the Light of the World: The Biblical Understanding of Light and Darkness," *Interpretation*, Vol. 17 (1963), pp. 439–449.

Allen, E. L., "The Jewish Christian Church in the Fourth Gospel," *Journal of Biblical Literature*, Vol. 74 (1955), pp. 88–92.

Barrett, C. K., *The Gospel According to St. John*. London: S.P.C.K., 1958.

———, "The Holy Spirit in the Fourth Gospel," *Journal of Theological Studies*, N.S., Vol. 1 (1950), pp. 1–15.

———, "The Place of Eschatology in the Fourth Gospel," *Expository Times*, Vol. 59 (1947–1948), pp. 302–305.

———, *The Prologue of St. John's Gospel*. London: The Athlone Press, 1971.

———, "The Theological Vocabulary of the Fourth Gospel and of the Gospel of Truth," in W. Klassen and G. F. Snyder (eds.), *Current Issues in New Testament Interpretation*. Harper & Brothers, 1962. Pp. 210–223.

Barrosse, Thomas, "The Relationship of Love to Faith in St. John," *Theological Studies*, Vol. 18 (1957), pp. 538–559.

Behm, J., "Paraklētos," *TDNT*, Vol. V, pp. 800–814.

Bernard, J. H., *A Critical and Exegetical Commentary on the Gospel According to St. John.* 2 vols. Edinburgh: T. & T. Clark, 1928.

Bianchi, Ugo (ed.), *The Origins of Gnosticism.* Leiden: E. J. Brill, 1967.

Borgen, Peder, "Logos Was the True Light," *Novum Testamentum*, Vol. 14 (1972), pp. 115–130.

———, "Observations on the Targumic Character of the Prologue of John," *New Testament Studies*, Vol. 16 (1969–1970), pp. 288–295.

Bowen, C. R., "Love in the Fourth Gospel," *Journal of Religion*, Vol. 13 (1933), pp. 39–49.

Brown, F.; Driver, S. R., and Briggs, C. A. (eds.), *A Hebrew and English Lexicon of the Old Testament.* Oxford: At the Clarendon Press [1907], 1959.

Brown, Raymond E., *The Gospel According to John*, Vol. I (i–xii) and Vol. II (xiii–xxi). Doubleday & Company, Inc., 1966, 1970.

———, "The Gospel of Thomas and St. John's Gospel," *New Testament Studies*, Vol. 9 (1962–1963), pp. 155–177.

———, "The Kerygma of the Gospel According to John: The Johannine View of Jesus in Modern Studies," *Interpretation*, Vol. 21 (1967), pp. 387–400.

———, "The Paraclete in the Fourth Gospel," *New Testament Studies*, Vol. 13 (1966–1967), pp. 113–132.

———, "The 'Paraclete' in the Light of Modern Research," in *Studia Evangelica*, Vol. IV. Berlin: Akademie-Verlag, 1968. Pp. 158–165.

———, *New Testament Essays.* Doubleday & Company, Inc., Image Books, 1968.

Brown, R. Percival, "*Entolē Kainē* (St. John 13:34)," *Theology*, Vol. 26 (April 1933), pp. 184–193.

Brownlee, W. H., "The Dead Sea Manual of Discipline: Translation and Notes," *Bulletin of the American Schools of Oriental Research*, Supplementary Studies, Nos. 10–12. New Haven: American Schools of Oriental Research, 1951.

Bruce, F. F., *Second Thoughts on the Dead Sea Scrolls.* Wm. B. Eerdmans Publishing Company, 1956.

Büchsel, F., *"Eimi,"* *TDNT*, Vol. II, pp. 398–400.

———, *"Monogenēs,"* *TDNT*, Vol. IV, pp. 737–741.

Bultmann, Rudolf, *"Alētheia,"* *TDNT*, Vol. I, pp. 232–251.

———, *"Ginōskō,"* *TDNT*, Vol. I, pp. 689–719.

———, *The Gospel of John.* The Westminster Press, 1971.

———, *Jesus and the Word.* Charles Scribner's Sons, 1958.

———, *"Pisteuō,"* *TDNT*, Vol. VI, pp. 222–228.

———, *Theology of the New Testament,* Vol. II. Charles Scribner's Sons, 1955.

———, *"Zaō,* John's View of Life as Present," *TDNT,* Vol. II, pp. 870 872.

Burrows, Millar, *The Dead Sea Scrolls.* The Viking Press, Inc., 1955.

Cadman, W. H., *The Open Heaven: The Revelation of God in the Johannine Sayings of Jesus,* ed. by G. B. Caird. Oxford: Basil Blackwell & Mott, Ltd., 1969.

Casey, R. P., "Gnosis, Gnosticism, and the New Testament," in *The Background of the New Testament and Its Eschatology,* ed. by W. D. Davies and D. Daube. Cambridge: At the University Press, 1956. Pp. 52–80.

Charles, R. H., *The Apocrypha and Pseudepigrapha of the Old Testament in English.* 2 vols. Oxford: At the Clarendon Press, 1913.

Charlesworth, J. H., "A Critical Comparison of the Dualism in 1QS III,13–IV,26 and the 'Dualism' Contained in the Fourth Gospel," in J. H. Charlesworth (ed.), *John and Qumran.* London: Geoffrey Chapman Publishers, 1972. Pp. 76–105.

Colwell, E. C., and Titus, E. L., *The Gospel of the Spirit.* Harper & Brothers, 1953.

Conzelmann, H., *An Outline of the Theology of the New Testament.* Harper & Row, Publishers, Inc., 1969.

Correll, Alf, *Consummatum Est: Eschatology and Church in the Gospel of St. John.* London: S.P.C.K., 1958.

Coutts, J., "The Messianic Secret in St. John's Gospel," in *Studia Evangelica,* Vol. III. Berlin: Akademie-Verlag, 1964. Pp. 45–57.

Cross, F. M., *The Ancient Library of Qumran and Modern Biblical Studies.* Doubleday & Company, Inc., 1958.

Cullmann, Oscar, *The Christology of the New Testament.* The Westminster Press, 1959.

———, "The Gospel According to St. John and Early Christian

Worship," in his *Early Christian Worship* (Studies in Biblical Theology, No. 10). London: SCM Press, Ltd., 1953. Pp. 37–119.

Dahl, N. A., "The Johannine Church and History," in W. Klassen and G. F. Snyder (eds.), *Current Issues in New Testament Interpretation*. Harper & Brothers, 1962. Pp. 124–142.

Daube, D., "The 'I Am' of the Messianic Presence," in *The New Testament and Rabbinic Judaism*. London: Athlone Press, 1956. Pp. 325–329.

Davey, J. E., *The Jesus of St. John*. London: Lutterworth Press, 1958.

Davies, W. D., " 'Knowledge' in the Dead Sea Scrolls and Matthew 11:25–30," *Harvard Theological Review,* Vol. 46 (July, 1953), pp. 113–139.

———, "Paul and the Dead Sea Scrolls: Flesh and Spirit," in Krister Stendahl (ed.), *The Scrolls and the New Testament*. Harper & Brothers, 1957. Pp. 157–182.

De Kruijf, T. C., "The Glory of the Only Son (John 1:14)," in *Studies in John*. Leiden: E. J. Brill, 1970.

Dodd, C. H., *The Bible and the Greeks*. London: Hodder & Stoughton, Ltd., 1935.

———, "Eternal Life," in C. H. Dodd, *New Testament Studies*. Manchester University Press, 1953. Pp. 160–173.

———, *Historical Tradition in the Fourth Gospel*. Cambridge: At the University Press, 1963.

———, *The Interpretation of the Fourth Gospel*. Cambridge: At the University Press, 1958.

Evans, Ernest, "The Verb *agapan* in the Fourth Gospel," in F. L. Cross (ed.), *Studies in the Fourth Gospel*. London: A. R. Mowbray & Company, Ltd., 1957. Pp. 64–71.

Feuillet, André, "The Era of the Church in St. John," *Theology Digest,* Vol. 11 (1963), pp. 3–10.

———, *Johannine Studies*. Alba House, 1964.

Filson, Floyd V., "The Gospel of Life: A Study of the Gospel of John," in W. Klassen and G. F. Snyder (eds.), *Current Issues in New Testament Interpretation*. Harper & Brothers, 1962. Pp. 111–123.

Freed, E. D., "The Manner of Worship in John 4:32 f.," in J. M. Myers and others (eds.), *Search the Scriptures*. Leiden: E. J. Brill, 1969. Pp. 33–48.

————, "The Son of Man in the Fourth Gospel," *Journal of Biblical Literature*, Vol. 86 (1967), pp. 402–409.

Fuller, Reginald H., *The Foundations of New Testament Christology*. Charles Scribner's Sons, 1965.

Furnish, Victor Paul, "The Johannine Literature: Love One Another," in V. P. Furnish, *The Love Command in the New Testament*. Abingdon Press, 1972. Pp. 132–158.

Gaffney, J., "Believing and Knowing in the Fourth Gospel," *Theological Studies*, Vol. 26 (1965), pp. 215–241.

Grant, Robert M., *A Historical Introduction to the New Testament*. Harper & Row, Publishers, Inc., 1963.

Grillmeier, Aloys, *Christ in Christian Tradition*. Sheed & Ward, 1965.

Grossouw, W., *Revelation and Redemption: A Sketch of the Theology of St. John*. The Newman Press, 1955.

Hahn, F., *The Titles of Jesus in Christology*. London: Lutterworth Press, 1969.

Harner, Philip B., *The "I am" of the Fourth Gospel: A Study in Johannine Usage and Thought*. Fortress Press, 1970.

Harrelson, Walter, "The Idea of *Agape* in the New Testament," *Journal of Religion*, Vol. 31 (July, 1951), pp. 169–182.

Harris, J. Rendel, *The Odes and Psalms of Solomon*. Cambridge: At the University Press, 1911.

————, *The Origin of the Prologue to St. John's Gospel*. Cambridge: At the University Press, 1917.

Hawthorne, G. F., "The Concept of Faith in the Fourth Gospel," *Bibliotheca Sacra*, Vol. 116 (1959), pp. 117–126.

Hendriksen, W., *Exposition of the Gospel According to John*. 2 vols. Baker Book House, 1953.

Higgins, A. J. B., *Jesus and the Son of Man*. London: Lutterworth Press, 1964.

Hort, F. J. A., *The Christian Ecclesia*. London: Macmillan & Co., Ltd., 1900.

Hoskyns, E., and Davey, F. N., *The Fourth Gospel*, 2d ed. London: Faber & Faber, Ltd., 1947.

Howard, W. F., *Christianity According to St. John*. The Westminster Press, 1946.

Hunter, A. M., *According to John: The New Look at the Fourth Gospel*. The Westminster Press, 1968.

Jeremias, Joachim, *The Problem of the Historical Jesus.* Fortress Press, 1964.

Johnston, George, *The Spirit-Paraclete in the Gospel of John.* Cambridge: At the University Press, 1970.

Käsemann, Ernst, *New Testament Questions of Today.* Fortress Press, 1969.

——, *The Testament of Jesus.* Fortress Press, 1968.

Kittel, G., and others, *"Legō," TDNT,* Vol. IV, pp. 124–136.

Knox, John, *The Humanity and Divinity of Christ.* Cambridge: At the University Press, 1967.

Koch, G. A., "An Investigation of the Possible Relationship Between the Gospel of John and the Sectarian Documents of the Dead Sea Scrolls." Unpublished thesis. Philadelphia: Eastern Baptist Theological Seminary, 1959.

Kraft, Robert A., *Barnabas and the Didache.* Vol. III of *The Apostolic Fathers,* ed. by Robert M. Grant. Thomas Nelson & Sons, 1965.

Kuhn, Karl Georg, "New Light on Temptation, Sin, and Flesh in the New Testament," in Krister Stendahl (ed.), *The Scrolls and the New Testament.* Harper & Brothers, 1957. Pp. 94–113.

Kysar, Robert, "The Background of the Prologue of the Fourth Gospel: A Critique of Historical Methods," *Canadian Journal of Theology,* Vol. 16 (1970), pp. 250–255.

Leaney, A. R. C., "The Johannine Paraclete and the Qumran Scrolls," in J. H. Charlesworth (ed.), *John and Qumran.* London: Geoffrey Chapman Publishers, 1972. Pp. 38–61.

Lee, E. K., *The Religious Thought of St. John.* London: S.P.C.K., 1950.

Liddell, H. G., and Scott, Robert (compilers), *A Greek-English Lexicon,* 9th ed. Oxford: At the Clarendon Press, 1940.

Lindars, Barnabas, *Behind the Fourth Gospel.* London: S.P.C.K., 1971.

——, *The Gospel of John.* London: Oliphants, Ltd., 1972.

Lofthouse, W. F., *The Father and the Son: A Study in Johannine Thought.* London: SCM Press, Ltd., 1934.

——, "Father and Sonship in the Fourth Gospel," *Expository Times,* Vol. 43 (1931–1932), pp. 442–448.

Lyons, Damian B., "The Concept of Eternal Life in the Gospel

According to Saint John." Unpublished dissertation. Washington, D.C.: The Catholic University of America, 1938.

Macgregor, G. H. C., *The Gospel of John.* Harper & Brothers, 1929.

McIntyre, John, *The Shape of Christology.* London: SCM Press, Ltd., 1966.

McKelvey, R. J., *The New Temple: The Church in the New Testament.* Oxford University Press, 1969.

MacRae, George W., "The Ego-Proclamation in Gnostic Sources," in E. Bammel, *The Trial of Jesus.* London: SCM Press, Ltd., 1970. Pp. 122–134.

Manson, T. W., *On Paul and John* (Studies in Biblical Theology, No. 38). London: SCM Press, Ltd., 1963.

Manson, W., "The EGO EIMI of the Messianic Presence in the New Testament," *Journal of Theological Studies*, Vol. 48 (1947), pp. 137–145.

Marshall, I. H., "The Divine Sonship of Jesus," *Interpretation*, Vol. 21 (1967), pp. 87–103.

Martyn, J. Louis, *History and Theology in the Fourth Gospel.* Harper & Row, Publishers, Inc., 1968.

Moody, Dale, "God's Only Son: The Translation of John 3:16 in the Revised Standard Version," *Journal of Biblical Literature*, Vol. 72 (1953), pp. 213–219.

Morris, Leon, *The Gospel According to John.* Wm. B. Eerdmans Publishing Company, 1971.

———, *Studies in the Fourth Gospel.* Wm. B. Eerdmans Publishing Company, 1969.

Moule, C. F. D., "The Individualism of the Fourth Gospel," *Novum Testamentum*, Vol. 5 (1962), pp. 171–190.

Mussner, Franz, *The Historical Jesus in the Gospel of St. John*, tr. by W. J. O'Hara. Herder & Herder, Inc., 1967.

Pancaro, Severino, " 'People of God' in St. John's Gospel?" *New Testament Studies*, Vol. 16 (1970), pp. 114–129.

Phillips, G. L., "Faith and Vision in the Fourth Gospel," in F. L. Cross (ed.), *Studies in the Fourth Gospel.* London: A. R. Mowbray & Co., Ltd., 1957. Pp. 83–96.

Pollard, T. E., *Johannine Christology and the Early Church.* Cambridge: At the University Press, 1970.

Pope, R., "Faith and Knowledge in Pauline and Johannine Thought," *Expository Times*, Vol. 41 (1929–1930), pp. 421–427.

Price, James L., "Light from Qumran Upon Some Aspects of Johannine Theology," in J. H. Charlesworth (ed.), *John and Qumran*. London: Geoffrey Chapman Publishers, 1972. Pp. 9–37.

Puech, H. C.; Quispel, G.; and van Unnik, W. V., *The Jung Codex: A Newly Recovered Gnostic Papyrus*, tr. and ed. by F. L. Cross. London: A. R. Mowbray & Co., Ltd., 1955.

Quell, G., and others, *"Agapaō," TDNT,* Vol. I, pp. 21–55.

Ringgren, Helmer, *Word and Wisdom. Studies in the Hypostatization of Divine Qualities and Functions in the Ancient Near East.* Lund: H. Ohlssons boktryckerei, 1947.

Roberts, J. W., "Some Observations on the Meaning of 'Eternal Life' in the Gospel of John," *Restoration Quarterly*, Vol. 7 (1963), pp. 186–193.

Robinson, J. A. T., "The New Look on the Fourth Gospel," in his *Twelve New Testament Studies* (Studies in Biblical Theology, No. 34). London: SCM Press, Ltd., 1962. Pp. 94–106.

Sanders, Jack T., *The New Testament Christological Hymns.* Cambridge: At the University Press, 1971.

Sanders, Joseph N., *A Commentary on the Gospel According to John*, ed. and completed by B. A. Mastin. Harper & Row, Publishers, Inc., 1968.

———, "John, Gospel of," *The Interpreter's Dictionary of the Bible*, ed. by G. A. Buttrick and others. Vol. E-J. Abingdon Press, 1962. Pp. 932–946.

Schnackenburg, R., "The Church in the Johannine Writings Including the Apocalypse," in his *The Church in the New Testament*, tr. by W. J. O'Hara. Herder & Herder, Inc., 1965. Pp. 103–117.

———, *The Gospel According to St. John*, Vol. I. Herder & Herder, Inc., 1968.

Schrenk, G., *"Entolē," TDNT,* Vol. II, pp. 553–555.

———, *"Patēr," TDNT,* Vol. V, pp. 996–1003.

Schweizer, Eduard, "The Concept of the Church in the Gospel and Epistles of St. John," in A. J. B. Higgins (ed.), *New Testament Essays* (studies in memory of T. W. Manson). Manchester University Press, 1959. Pp. 230–245.

———, "John's Conception of the Church, and Its Development," in Eduard Schweizer, *Church Order in the New Testament* (Studies in Biblical Theology, No. 32). London: SCM Press, Ltd., 1961. Pp. 117–138.

———, "The Son of Man Again," *New Testament Studies*, Vol. 9 (1963), pp. 256–261.

———, and others, *"Huios," TDNT*, Vol. VIII, pp. 334–400.

———, and others, *"Pneuma," TDNT*, Vol. VI, pp. 332–455.

Scott, E. F., *The Fourth Gospel: Its Purpose and Theology*. Edinburgh: T. & T. Clark. 2d ed., 1908.

Sidebottom, E. M., *The Christ of the Fourth Gospel*. London: S.P.C.K., 1961.

Simon, U. E., "Eternal Life in the Fourth Gospel," in F. L. Cross (ed.), *Studies in the Fourth Gospel*. London: A. R. Mowbray & Company, Ltd., 1957. Pp. 97–109.

Smalley, Stephen S., "The Johannine Son of Man Sayings," *New Testament Studies*, Vol. 15 (1968–1969), pp. 278–301.

Smith, T. C., "The Christology of the Fourth Gospel," *Review and Expositor*, Vol. 71 (1974), pp. 19–30.

Snyder, Graydon F., *The Shepherd of Hermas* (Vol. VI of *The Apostolic Fathers*, ed. by Robert M. Grant). Thomas Nelson & Sons, 1968.

Spicq, Ceslaus, *Agape in the New Testament*, Vol. III (*Agape in the Gospel, Epistles, and Apocalypse of St. John*, tr. by M. A. McNamara and M. H. Richter). B. Herder Book Co., 1966.

Stauffer, Ethelbert, *"Egō," TDNT*, Vol. II, pp. 343–362.

———, *Jesus and His Story*. Alfred A. Knopf, Inc., 1960.

Strachan, R. H., *The Fourth Gospel: Its Significance and Environment*, 3d ed. London: SCM Press, Ltd., 1941.

Summers, R., "The Johannine View of the Future Life," *Review and Expositor*, Vol. 58 (1961), pp. 331–347.

Taylor, Vincent, *The Names of Jesus*. London: The Macmillan Company, 1953.

TDNT. Theological Dictionary of the New Testament, ed. by G. Kittel and G. Friedrich; 9 vols., tr. by G. W. Bromiley. Wm. B. Eerdmans Publishing Company, 1964–1974.

Thomas, R. W., "The Meaning of the Terms 'Life' and 'Death' in the Fourth Gospel and in Paul," *Scottish Journal of Theology*, Vol. 21 (1968), pp. 199–212.

Tietze, G., "The Knowledge of God in the Fourth Gospel," *Journal of Bible and Religion*, Vol. 22 (1954), pp. 14–19.

Titus, Eric L., *The Message of the Fourth Gospel.* Abingdon Press, 1957.

Turner, W., "Believing and Everlasting Life—A Johannine Inquiry," *Expository Times*, Vol. 64 (1952–1953), pp. 50–52.

Van den Bussche, H., "The Church in the Fourth Gospel," in Jean Giblet and others, *The Birth of the Church: A Biblical Study*, tr. by C. U. Quinn. Alba House, 1968. Pp. 83–109.

Vanderlip, D. G., "A Comparative Study of Certain Alleged Similarities Between the Literature of Qumran and the Fourth Gospel." Unpublished dissertation. Los Angeles: University of Southern California, 1959.

Van Unnik, W. C., "The Purpose of St. John's Gospel," in *Studia Evangelica*, Vol. I. Berlin: Akademie-Verlag, 1959. Pp. 382–411.

Vawter, Bruce, "Johannine Theology," in *The Jerome Biblical Commentary*, ed. by R. E. Brown, J. A. Fitzmyer, and R. E. Murphy. Prentice-Hall, Inc., 1968. Pp. 828–839.

————, "Some Recent Developments in Johannine Theology," *Biblical Theology Bulletin*, 1971, pp. 30–58.

Vermès, G., *The Dead Sea Scrolls in English.* Penguin Books, Inc., 1962.

Via, D. O., Jr., "Darkness, Christ, and the Church in the Fourth Gospel," *Scottish Journal of Theology*, Vol. 14 (1961), pp. 172–193.

Weisengoff, J. P., "The Acquisition, Maintenance and Recovery of Life According to St. John," *Ecclesiastical Review*, Vol. 104 (1941), pp. 492–505.

————, "Light and Its Relation to Life in Saint John," *Catholic Biblical Quarterly*, Vol. 8 (1946), pp. 448–451.

Wernle, Paul, *The Beginnings of Christianity*, Vol. II, tr. by G. A. Bienemann. G. P. Putnam's Sons, 1904.

Wilson, R. McL., "Gnostic Origins," *Vigiliae Christianae*, Vol. 9 (November, 1955), pp. 193–211.

Windisch, Hans, *The Spirit-Paraclete in the Fourth Gospel*, tr. by J. W. Cox. Fortress Press, 1968.

Part II. Titles in Other Languages

Alanen, Yrjö, "Das Wahrheitsproblem in der Bibel und in der griechischen Philosophie," *Kerygma und Dogma*, Vol. 3 (1957), pp. 230–239.

Bammel, Ernst, "Jesus und der Paraklet in Johannes 16," in B. Lindars and S. S. Smalley, *Christ and Spirit in the New Testament*. Cambridge: At the University Press, 1973. Pp. 199–217.

Betz, Otto, *Der Paraklet*. Leiden: E. J. Brill, 1963.

Blank, Josef, "Der johanneische Wahrheits-Begriff," *Biblische Zeitschrift*, Vol. 7 (1963), pp. 163–173.

Böcher, Otto, *Der johanneische Dualismus im Zusammenhang des nachbiblischen Judentums*. Gütersloh, 1965.

Boismard, M. E., "La Connaissance dans l'alliance nouvelle, d'après la première lettre de saint Jean," *Revue Biblique*, Vol. 56 (1949), pp. 365–391.

Bonnard, P., "Connaître Dieu selon le quatrième évangile et la gnose hellénistique," *Foi et Vie*, Vol. 64 (1965), pp. 483–492.

Bornkamm, G., "Der Paraklet im Johannesevangelium," in Festschrift Rudolf Bultmann zum 65 Geburtstag überreicht. Stuttgart: Kohlhammer, 1949. Pp. 12–35.

Braun, F.-M., *Jean le Théologien. Sa théologie; le Christ, notre seigneur, hier, aujourd'hui, toujours*. Paris: Libraire Lecoffre, 1972.

Büchsel, F., *Der Begriff der Wahrheit in dem Evangelium und den Briefen des Johannes*. Gütersloh, 1911.

Casalis, M., "Le Thème de la connaissance de Dieu dans les milieux littéraires essénien, paulinien et johannique," *Foi et Vie*, Vol. 64 (1965), pp. 493–522.

Cullmann, Oscar, "L'Evangile johannique et l'histoire du salut," *New Testament Studies*, Vol. 11 (1964–1965), pp. 111–122.

de la Potterie, I., "L'Arrière-fond du thème johannique de vérité," in *Studia Evangelica*, Vol. I. Berlin: Akademie-Verlag, 1959. Pp. 277–294.

———, "Oida et ginōskō. Les Deux Modes de la connaissance dans le quatrième évangile," *Biblica*, Vol. 40 (1959), pp. 709–725.

Durr, Lorenz, *Die Wertung des göttlichen Wortes im Alten Testament und im antiken Orient*. Leipzig, 1938.

Feuillet, André, "Les *Ego eimi* christologiques du quatrième évangile," *Recherches de Science Religieuse*, Vol. 54 (1966), pp. 5–22, 213–240.

Frey, J. B., "Le Concept de 'vie' dans l'évangile de saint Jean," *Biblica*, Vol. I (1920), pp. 37–58, 211–239.

Haenchen, E., "Probleme des johanneischen 'Prologs,'" *Zeitschrift für Theologie und Kirche*, Vol. 60 (1963), pp. 305–334.

Irigoin, Jean, "La Composition rythmique du prologue de Jean (1:1–18)," *Revue Biblique*, Vol. 88 (1971), pp. 501–514.

Jeremias, Jaochim, *Der Prolog des Johannesevangeliums*. Stuttgart: Calwer Verlag, 1967.

Koole, J. L., "Diorama Johanneum. *Zōē*," *Gereformeerd Theologisch Tijdschrift*, Vol. 43 (1942), pp. 276–284.

Mowinckel, S., "Die Vorstellungen des Spätjudentums vom heiligen Geist als Fürsprecher und der johanneische Paraklet," *Zeitschrift für die neutestamentliche Wissenschaft und die Kunde der älteren Kirche*, Vol. 32 (1933), pp. 97–130.

Mussner, Franz, "Die johanneischen Parakletsprüche und die apostolische Tradition," *Biblische Zeitschrift*, Vol. 5 (1961), pp. 56–70.

———, "*Zōē*. Die Anschauung vom 'Leben' im vierten Evangelium unter Berücksichtigung der Johannesbriefe," *Münchener Theologische Studien*, Vol. 1, No. 5 (1952), pp. v–xv, 1–190.

Richter, G., "Die Fleischwerdung des Logos im Johannesevangelium," *Novum Testamentum*, Vol. 13 (1971), pp. 81–126; Vol. 14 (1972), pp. 257–276.

Schlatter, A., *Der Glaube in Neuen Testament*, 5th ed., Stuttgart: Calwer Verlag, 1963.

Schlier, H., *Besinnung auf das Neue Testament*. Freiburg: Verlag Herder, 1964.

———, *Das Ende der Zeit*. Vol. III. Freiburg: Verlag Herder, 1971.

Schnackenburg, R., "Die 'Anbetung in Geist und Wahrheit' (Joh. 4:23) im Lichte von Qumran-Texten," *Biblische Zeitschrift*, Vol. 3 (1959), pp. 88–94.

———, *Die Johannesbriefe*. Freiburg: Verlag Herder, 1963.

———, *Das Johannesevangelium*, Vol. II. Freiburg: Verlag Herder, 1971.

———, "Der Menschensohn im Johannesevangelium," *New Testament Studies*, Vol. 11 (1964–1965), pp. 123–137.

————, "Zum Begriff der 'Wahrheit' in den beiden kleinen Johannesbriefen," *Biblische Zeitschrift*, Vol. 11 (1967), pp. 253–258.

Schultz, S., *Komposition und Herkunft der johanneischen Reden*. Stuttgart: Verlag W. Kohlhammer, 1960.

————, *Untersuchungen zur Menschensohn-Christologie im Johannesevangelium*. Göttingen: Vandenhoeck & Ruprecht, 1957.

Schweizer, Eduard, *Ego eimi*. Göttingen: Vandenhoeck, 1939.

————, "Das johanneische Zeugnis vom Herrenmahl," *Evangelische Theologie*, Vol. 12 (1952–1953), pp. 341–363.

Sevenster, G., *De Christologie van het Nieuwe Testament*. Uitgeversmaatschappij te Amsterdam, 1948.

Smilde, E., *Leven in de Johanneïsche Geschriften*. Kampen: J. H. Kok, 1943.

Wenz, H., "Sehen und Glauben bei Johannes," *Theologische Zeitschrift* (Basel), Vol. 17 (1961), pp. 17–25.

Zimmermann, H., "Das absolute *Ego eimi* als die neutestamentliche Offenbarungsformel," *Biblische Zeitschrift*, Vol. 4 (1960), pp. 54–69, 266–276.

Indexes

SUBJECT INDEX

Authorship, 26 ff.
Baptism, 88 ff.
Believe, 17, 95 ff., 107 f.
Christology, 17 ff., 43 f., 46 ff.,
    58 ff., 92
Church, 22, 72 ff.
Darkness, 133 ff.
Date of John's Gospel, 26 f.
Dead Sea Scrolls, 114 ff.,
    140 ff., 157 f., 161 f.
Discourses, 129, 178 ff.
Dualism, 111, 133 ff.
Epilogue, 24 f.
Eschatology, 38 ff., 172
Evangelism, 20, 23, 128 ff.
Flesh (vs. spirit), 136 f.
Freedom, 12 f.
Glory, 48 ff.
Gnosticism, 23 f., 52, 90,
    109 ff., 133 ff., 146 ff., 158
God (revelation of), 15 f.,
    18 f., 47 ff., 97, 108
Grace, 103, 159 f.
History, 174 ff.
Holy Spirit, 15 f., 82 f., 155 f.,
    161 f., 164 ff., 180
"I am" sayings, 65 ff., 176 f.

Instruction, 128 ff.
John the Baptist, 23, 89
John, First Letter of, 25 f.
Judaism, 20 f., 91 ff., 99 f.,
    129, 138 f., 162 f.
Kingdom of God, 41 ff., 135,
    145 f.
Know, 95, 101, 104 ff.
Life, 10 f., 17 f., 31 ff., 102,
    104
Light, 133 ff.
Lord's Supper, 88 ff.
Love, 12 ff., 118 ff.
Mandaeism, 68, 78, 110, 167
Prologue, 47 ff.
Purpose of writer, 16 ff., 28,
    46, 96 f., 128
Signs, 129, 131, 178
Son of God, 19, 54, 60 ff.
Son of Man, 47 f., 58 ff.
Truth, 12 ff., 153 ff.
Union with God, 108 f.
Unity, 83 f.
Wisdom, 52 ff., 64, 158
Word, 46 ff.
World, 10, 93 f., 124 ff., 133 ff.
Worship, 160 f.

217

Author Index

Aalen, S., 199
Alanen, Yrjö, 157

Bammel, Ernst, 200
Barrett, C. K., 20, 38, 39, 56, 113, 191, 192, 193, 194, 197, 200
Blank, Josef, 158
Bonnard, P., 106
Bowen, C. R., 196
Briggs, C. A., 198
Brown, F., 198
Brown, Raymond E., 20, 55, 70, 83, 87, 97, 120, 143, 167, 175, 184, 187, 190, 191, 192, 199, 200
Brown, R. Percival, 196
Brownlee, W. H., 197
Bruce, F. F., 115
Büchsel, F., 64, 199
Bultmann, Rudolf, 52, 56, 68, 77, 78, 84, 85, 86, 88, 98, 99, 101, 107, 123, 160, 167, 174, 187, 194, 199
Burrows, Millar, 195

Cadman, W. H., 47, 60, 134
Caird, G. B., 197
Casalis, M., 195
Casey, R. P., 113, 194
Charles, R. H., 198
Charlesworth, J. H., 145, 198, 200
Clement of Alexandria, 28
Colwell, E. C., 48, 92, 144, 147, 176, 198, 200
Conzelmann, H., 52
Correll, Alf, 38, 158
Coutts, J., 62
Cross, F. L., 188, 195, 196

Cross, F. M., 200
Cullmann, Oscar, 51, 78, 93, 188, 190

Dahl, Nils, 78, 85
Daube, D., 194
Davey, F. N., 20, 175, 186, 193
Davies, W. D., 115, 151, 194
de la Potterie, I., 157, 158, 194
Dodd, C. H., 20, 52, 78, 108, 110, 111, 112, 156, 175, 182, 186, 191, 193, 195, 196, 198
Driver, S. R., 198
Durr, Lorenz, 55

Eusebius, 187
Evans, E., 121, 123

Feuillet, André, 68, 191
Filson, Floyd V., 114, 188
Freed, E. D., 190, 199
Furnish, V. P., 119

Grant, Robert M., 57

Harner, Philip B., 67, 68, 69
Harris, J. Rendel, 56
Hendriksen, W., 123, 196
Higgins, A. J. B., 59, 192
Hort, F. J. A., 192
Hoskyns, E., 20, 175, 186, 193
Howard, W. F., 127, 156, 157
Hunter, A. M., 201

Jeremias, Joachim, 52
Johnston, George, 200

Käsemann, Ernst, 48, 56, 59, 87, 124, 125

Klassen, W., 188, 192, 195
Koch, G. A., 199
Kraft, Robert A., 198
Kuhn, K. G., 143

Leaney, A. R. C., 168
Lee, E. K., 194, 196
Liddell, H. G., 198
Lindars, Barnabas, 69, 180, 182, 189, 200
Lofthouse, W. F., 63

Macgregor, G. H. C., 91
MacRae, George W., 191
Manson, W., 66
Marshall, I. H., 190
Martyn, J. Louis, 60, 184, 187, 193
Mastin, B. A., 176, 178, 183
Moody, Dale, 190
Morris, Leon, 64, 123, 177, 179, 193
Moule, C. F. D., 86, 87
Mowinckel, S., 200
Mussner, Franz, 32, 43, 103, 164, 174, 175, 177
Myers, J. M., 199

Oulton, J. E. L., 187

Pancaro, Severino, 191
Phillips, G. L., 98
Philo, 51, 52, 110, 156
Pollard, T. E., 54
Price, James L., 145, 198
Puech, H. C., 195

Quell, G., 120, 196

Ringgren, Heimer, 55

Sanders, Jack T., 55
Sanders, Joseph N., 146, 147, 176, 178, 183
Schlatter, A., 99
Schlier, H., 98, 103
Schnackenburg, R., 44, 45, 56, 60, 63, 68, 69, 85, 86, 102, 112, 135, 188, 191, 195, 199
Schrenk, G., 64, 119
Schultz, S., 189
Schweizer, Eduard, 62, 68, 85, 89, 192
Scott, E. F., 156, 192
Scott, R., 198
Sidebottom, E. M., 188, 189
Simon, U. E., 44
Smalley, S. S., 200
Smilde, E., 36
Snyder, G. F., 188, 192, 195, 198
Spicq, C., 121
Stauffer, E., 70, 196
Stendahl, K., 197, 198
Strachan, R. H., 178

Titus, E. L., 48, 92, 144, 147, 176, 197, 198

Vanderlip, D. G., 195
van Unnik, W. C., 20, 22
Vawter, Bruce, 200
Vermès, G., 197
Via, Dan O., Jr., 192

Wenz, H., 99
Wernle, Paul, 128
Wilson, R. McL., 110, 111

Zimmermann, H., 68, 69

Scripture Index

Genesis
1:1 50
1:2 170
28:12 47
32:10 156
41:38 170
47:29 ... 156, 199
49 83

Exodus
3:14 67
34:6 157

Deuteronomy
13:13 74
14:1 75

Joshua
2:14 199

Judges
6:34 170
9:16 199
9:19 199

I Samuel
2:12 106

II Samuel
2:6 199
23:2 170

II Chronicles
31:20 199

Nehemiah
9:33 199

Psalms
23:1 78
25:10 159
36:10 107
51:11 170
74:1 78

78:52 78
78:70 ff. 78
80:8 ff. ... 79, 159
100:3 78
111:8 199
139:7 170

Proverbs
3:19 54
8:12 52
8:23 52
8:29 f. 52

Isaiah
1:2 75
5:1 ff. ... 79, 159
5:7 79
27:2 ff. 79
40:11 78
41:4 67
43:10 67
43:13 67
43:25 67

Jeremiah
2:8 159
2:21 ..... 79, 159
10:20 75
10:21 159
12:10 159
23:1 ff. .. 78, 160
31:10 78
31:31 ff. 194

Ezekiel
15:2 ff. 159
19:10 ff. 159
34 78
34:1 ff. 160

Daniel
7:13 47

Hosea
1:10 75
11:1 159

Amos
8:10 64

Zechariah
12:10 64

Matthew
1:1 50
5:14 149
5:16 149
7:24 65
7:28 f. 65
11:25 ff. 195
11:27 63
19:16 f. 40
22:16 154
24:5 65
24:36 63
28:19 63
28:19 f. 80

Mark
3:17 74
6:50 70
9:43 42
9:45 42
9:47 42
12:14 154
13:6 70
13:32 63
14:62 70

Luke
1:2 82
3:38 50
5:1 ff. 80
5:10 80
10:22 63

10:29 ff. 128
12:15 40
16:8 149
16:11 154
16:25 40
18:29 f. 41
21:8 70
22:20 120
22:70 70
24:21 49
24:39 70

John
1:1 .... 50, 54
1:3 54
1:4 ...... 13, 34
1:4 f. 54
1:5 .... 136, 137
1:8 23
1:9 .. 13, 126, 159
1:11 ..... 76, 139
1:12 ..... 73, 80
1:13 .... 74, 137
1:14 .. 18, 24, 48,
51, 53, 54, 62,
64, 146, 154,
157, 159
1:17 .... 54, 100,
139, 154
1:18 .. 53, 60, 62,
63, 64
1:24 ff. 89
1:29 127
1:32 f. 164
1:33 89
1:34 ..... 60, 62
1:38 187
1:41 187
1:49 60
1:51 .. 47, 48, 58,
134
2:19 ff. 139

2:22 171
3:2 134
3:3 .. 41, 74, 135
3:5 ... 41, 88, 89,
168
3:6 137
3:7 135
3:8 ... 74, 93, 135
3:13 .. 47, 58, 59,
134, 135
3:13 ff. 61
3:14 58
3:14 f. 60
3:15 f. 37, 41
3:16 .. 14, 53, 60,
64, 80, 120,
121, 125, 126,
190
3:16 f. 35, 60,
124
3:17 .... 60, 127
3:18 .. 53, 60, 62,
64
3:18 f. 37
3:19 ... 122, 126,
137
3:21 ... 155, 156,
161
3:22 89
3:23 89
3:25 23
3:29 73
3:31 .... 134, 135
3:35 .. 60, 61, 122
3:36 .. 33, 36, 60
4:1 89
4:1 f. 89
4:2 89
4:10 .. 31, 34, 136
4:14 38
4:21 139
4:21 ff. 100

4:22 ..... 78, 163
4:23 199
4:23 f. 155
4:24 ... 127, 160
4:26 65
4:32 f. 199
4:35 .... 80, 126
4:36 38
4:42 .. 10, 80, 126
5:4 30
5:19 ..... 60, 61
5:20 .... 60, 122
5:21 .. 34, 60, 137
5:22 60
5:23 60
5:24 .. 33, 36, 37
5:24 f. 137
5:25 ..... 60, 98
5:26 ..... 34, 60
5:27 ..... 58, 60
5:28 f. 38
5:33 155
5:39 38
5:39 f. 33
6 91
6:4 187
6:11 91
6:20 ..... 65, 70
6:23 91
6:27 .. 38, 58, 60
6:29 ..... 99, 161
6:32 .... 100, 136,
139
6:32 ff. 91
6:33 126
6:33 ff. 134
6:35 .. 34, 65, 66
6:35 ff. 93
6:39 38
6:39 ff. 38
6:40 .. 37, 38, 60
6:41 ..... 65, 66

6:44 38
6:45 98
6:47 .. 37, 41, 92,
            93
6:48 65
6:51 .. 65, 66, 91
6:51 ff. 88, 93
6:53 .. 37, 58, 92
6:53 ff. 91, 92
6:54 .. 37, 38, 60
6:62 ..... 58, 59
6:63 .. 92, 93, 136,
            137
6:67 26
6:68 .. 34, 37, 102
6:68 f. 26, 97
6:69 107
7:39 82, 160, 164
7:53 ff. 30
8:12 .. 46, 65, 66,
            138
8:15 137
8:15 f. 137
8:18 65
8:23 .... 65, 133,
            135, 138
8:24 65
8:28 .. 58, 59, 65
8:31 ff. ... 102, 136
8:32 155
8:36 ...... 12, 60
8:40 155
8:42 ff. 136
8:44 ... 139, 155,
            162
8:44 f. 136
8:45 155
8:46 155
8:51 137
8:58 .. 65, 66, 67
9 184
9:4 138

9:5 .. 46, 66, 138
9:7 90
9:22 ...... 27, 94
9:35 58
9:35 ff. ... 60, 62,
            63
9:39 126
9:39 ff. 138
10:1 ff. 77
10:3 98
10:3 f. 77
10:4 ..... 77, 78
10:7 ..... 65, 66
10:8 98
10:9 ..... 65, 66
10:9 f. 36
10:10 .. 11, 17, 31,
        34, 44, 70, 136
10:11 .. 35, 65, 66,
            78, 159
10:14 ..... 65, 66
10:15 .... 35, 78
10:16 .. 10, 77, 78,
        83, 98, 127
10:17 35
10:27 98
10:28 37
10:33 62
10:36 .... 60, 62
10:38 67
10:40 89
11 34
11:3 122
11:4 60
11:5 122
11:9 f. 138
11:24 38
11:25 .. 34, 65, 66
11:25 f. 35
11:27 60
11:49 ff. 73
11:50 76

11:51 76
11:52 ..... 76, 80
12:16 171
12:20 f. 80
12:23 58
12:23 f. 60
12:24 12
12:25 .. 35, 38, 122
12:26 135
12:27 35
12:31 ... 125, 146
12:31 f. .. 136, 140
12:32 .... 80, 127
12:34 58
12:35 138
12:36 ..... 74, 75
12:42 ..... 27, 94
12:44 ff. 130
12:46 138
12:46 ff. 98
12:47 126
13 .... 29, 31
13–17 31
13–20 31
13:1 .. 76, 96, 127,
            131
13:2 ..... 91, 146
13:2 ff. 12
13:7 171
13:9 f. 90
13:12 ff. 12
13:14 f. 130
13:19 .. 65, 66, 67
13:23 122
13:27 146
13:30 138
13:31 58
13:33 75
13:34 .. 119, 120,
        124, 127, 130
13:34 f. 103
13:37 f. 35

14 29
14:2 39
14:2 f. 38
14:3 135
14:6 .. 13, 34, 36,
        46, 65, 66,
    100, 154, 157,
                163
14:7 .... 101, 105
14:9 101
14:9 ff. 18
14:13 60
14:16 160
14:16 ff. .. 82, 105,
    130, 160, 165
14:17 .. 101, 125,
    155, 161, 168
14:18 82
14:18 ff. 172
14:21 ... 122, 195
14:23 .... 39, 74,
    122, 169, 195
14:25 f. 165
14:26 .. 15, 82, 86,
                168
14:27 .. 102, 130
14:30 .. 29, 136,
                146
14:31 29
15 .... 29, 78
15–17 29
15:1 .. 13, 65, 66,
                159
15:4 .... 39, 130
15:4 ff. 79
15:5 .... 65, 66
15:5 f. 84
15:8 103
15:11 102
15:12 .. 119, 124,
        127, 130
15:13 35

15:16 81
15:17 .. 119, 124,
        127, 130
15:18 137
15:18 ff. .. 125, 130
15:19 .... 94, 135
15:20 94
15:26 .. 130, 155,
    161, 165, 168
15:26 f. .. 82, 86,
                171
15:27 130
16:2 .... 27, 94
16:7 155
16:7 ff. .. 82, 130,
                165
16:8 .. 165, 170
16:8 ff. .. 86, 165
16:11 .. 136, 146,
                165
16:12 ff. .. 82, 172,
        179, 180
16:13 .... 15, 82,
    155, 161, 168,
                171
16:13 ff. .. 86, 165
16:14 171
16:20 ff. 102
16:24 102
16:27 122
16:30 107
16:33 .. 94, 102,
    130, 135, 137,
                139
17 83
17:1 60
17:2 f. 37
17:3 .. 17, 34, 101,
        104, 108
17:4 83
17:6 .. 81, 135
17:8 107

17:11 .... 83, 130
17:12 81
17:13 102
17:14 94
17:16 135
17:17 155
17:19 155
17:20 80
17:20 ff. .. 26, 108
17:21 .... 83, 130
17:21 ff. 83
17:23 83
17:24 .. 37, 135
18 29
18:5 65
18:6 65
18:8 65
18:14 76
18:36 .. 41, 145
18:37 155
18:38 155
19:1 ff. 23
19:7 .. 60, 62
19:11 135
19:23 135
19:30 50
19:34 28
19:34 f. .. 88, 89,
                90
19:35 29
20:2 122
20:21 .. 80, 130
20:22 .. 82, 130,
                160
20:23 .. 85, 130
20:28 .. 62, 130
20:29 99
20:30 f. .. 16, 28,
    31, 35, 75,
        96, 180
20:31 .. 46, 54, 60,
                61

21 .... 24, 28, 29
21:1 ff. 80
21:3 80
21:3 ff. 130
21:15 ff. .. 85, 122,
                    130
21:17 124
21:19 ff. 130
21:20 ff. 28
21:21 ff. 130
21:22 38
21:23 28
21:24 .... 27, 28

Acts
4:23 77
9:2 75
11:26 75
24:23 77

Romans
7:9 f. 119
9:25 f. 76

I Corinthians
7:12 179
7:25 179
7:40 179
15:28 63

II Corinthians
6:14 f. 149

Galatians
4:19 75

Ephesians
5:9 f. 74
5:21 ff. 72

I Thessalonians
5:4 f. 148

I Timothy
3:1 ff. 87
5:8 77

Hebrews
1:2 63
1:8 63
3:6 63
5:8 63
7:28 63

I Peter
2:9 ...... 76, 81
2:9 f. 75

II Peter
1:21 170

I John
1:1 51
1:2 33
1:2 f. 34, 108
1:6 .... 155, 161
1:10 136
2:1 ...... 75, 165
2:2 165
2:4 136
2:12 75
2:19 ..... 26, 84
2:21 136
2:22 136
2:25 38
2:27 136
2:28 75
3:1 ...... 73, 74
3:2   37, 38, 40,
                    73
3:6 .... 101, 106

3:7 75
3:7 ff. 198
3:10 ...... 73, 74
3:16 35
3:17 f. 122
3:18 ..... 14, 75
4:1 ff. 198
4:2 f. 24
4:4 75
4:6 .... 168, 169
4:15 62
4:16 107
4:17 38
4:20 136
4:20 f. 45
5:2 73
5:4 100
5:5 62
5:6 90
5:8 90
5:11 33
5:12 ..... 43, 44
5:21 75

II John
1 85
4 161
7 24

III John
1 85
3 f. 161
9 85

Revelation
2 185
3 185
3:22 82
19:13 51
21:2 72